The
Quest
for the Stone

An Adventure in Archeology and Past Lives

JOSEPH PIO ASTERITA

authorHOUSE

AuthorHouse™
1663 Liberty Drive
Bloomington, IN 47403
www.authorhouse.com
Phone: 1 (800) 839-8640

Published by AuthorHouse   12/18/2015

ISBN: 978-1-5049-5466-2 (sc)
ISBN: 978-1-5049-5465-5 (e)

For my Family

Author's Note

Everybody loves a good adventure story, such as *Treasure Island* or *Raiders of the Lost Arc*. In this novel you meet a young archeologist, who through an unknown force travels back two-thousand years to discover himself, his lover and relives adventures beyond his wildest imaginings. *The Quest for the Stone* weaves time travel with quantum physics, adventure with archeology, the unknown with legend and ancient writings with the mystical. Here in is a multifaceted adventure story placed in interconnected time capsules of the present day and during the Roman invasion of England in the first century.

These are the aspects that weave in and out of the *Quest for the Stone*.

Julius Caesar led an expeditionary army in 55 BCE into Albion (ancient England), which he re-named Britannia. Caesar's army did not occupy the country but, with a show of force, persuaded the population to trade favorably with Rome. The trade relationship lasted into the next century. However, by 43 CE the independent minded Celts rejected the growing influence and pressure from Rome. In response and to fully gain the riches of Britannia and expand the empire, the Emperor

Claudius ordered the military invasion and occupation of Britannia. A sea invasion of four Roman legions comprised of soldiers and auxiliaries left Gaul (modern-day France) and landed in southeastern Britannia. It is during this invasion that the historical sections of our story take place. We join Legion II Augusta on its 10-year campaign to secure all lands in southern and western Britannia. Specifically, we are engaged with the legion's cavalry cohort as well as the Celtic population in what is now modern-day Somerset County. The topography of the ridge-like hill of the Great Beach Reserve southeast to the South Cadbury Hillfort is where our story unfolds. Archeological findings substantiate the Roman occupation in Somerset and, more importantly, the Hillfort is where evidence of a major conflict has been uncovered dating close to the time of the story. Roman remains have not yet been found on the Great Beach Reserve but because of its alluring landscape near Glastonbury and its strategic military location, it is the venue of our story.

There are legends galore emanating from ancient times, some based on evidence, others on lore, and some on both. For example, Mary Magdalene is believed by some to be the wife of Jesus. This is supported by recent finds in ancient scriptures while legend alludes to Mary bearing a daughter named Sarah. To avoid imprisonment and possible death, legend also states that Mary and Sarah left Palestine and traveled to southern France. They then journeyed to Britannia before the Roman invasion to commune with the Celtic Druids. In addition, there exists the Glastonbury legend of Joseph of Arimathea who settled there in 37 CE to start the first Christian community in Britannia. Our story's opening pages tells of Mary Magdalene meeting with the Druid High Priestess to unify their beliefs and experiences.

The introduction of Quantum Physics in the twentieth century has forever changed our scientific outlook on reality. Concepts such as countless parallel universes, multiple dimensions of existence, the entanglement of subatomic particles, and the ability to travel back in time stymie logical thought. The Theory of Traversable Wormholes explains how interstellar travel and time travel may be possible. Likewise, Astrophysics looks back in time by observing the light from stars and galaxies that are billions of years old. While the speed of light is the ultimate universal speed limit, the speed of the mind is infinitely faster. Can a time travel experience be attained in our deepest thoughts, imaginings or dreams? Perhaps guided by a higher self? Can we change or influence the past as we can the future?

The Abrahamic Religions while believing nature is the creation of a heavenly supreme deity give little or no role of nature spirits guiding the on-going functions and evolution of the earth. However, various earth-centered beliefs, specifically of Native Americans, support a spirit world intimately involved in nature under the guidance of a supreme deity. Likewise, Celtic beliefs refer to spirits who influence the air, earth, fire and water, which directly affect our lives. Christian mystics like St. Hildegard of Bingen wrote about their experiences with these spirits while St Francis of Assisi in *The Canticle of Brother Sun* tells how God works through nature to bless and sustain us. Our story combines these two belief systems - the Abrahamic and the Natural. Can this union provide a much-needed expansion in modern day spiritual (and scientific) beliefs?

Enjoy the story.

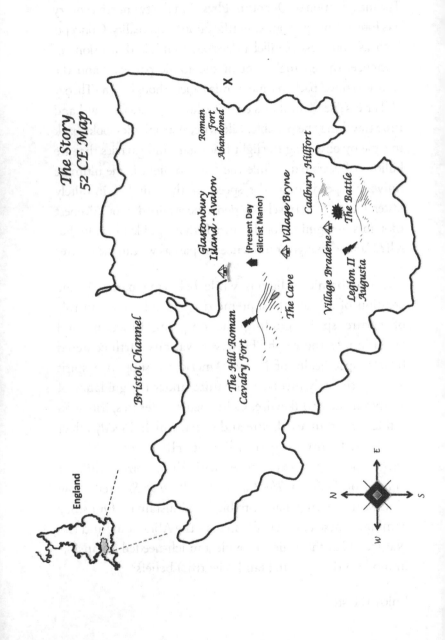

The Story
52 CE Map

England

Bristol Channel

Glastonbury
Island - Avalon

(Present Day
Gilcrist Manor)

The Hill - Roman
Cavalry Fort

The Cave

Village Bryne

Roman
Fort
Abandoned

Cadbury Hillfort

Village Bradene

Legion II
Augusta

The Battle

N   E
W   S

THE BEGINNING
37CE

Two women and two young girls stood facing each other at the center of the ancient Celtic village of Bryne in western Albion, south east of present day Glastonbury, England. Shadowed by the woman they were standing near, the girls looked at each other smiled and giggled. The women were nearly the same height but rather different in appearance. One dressed in a camel colored simple dress with a leather strap around her waist. Her olive skin and dark brown hair revealed her mid- eastern origin. Her eyes, soft and tender, reflected a loving gaze that spoke of a universe of deep caring. The other wore a woven green dress, flowers in her long flowing auburn hair, had light skin and wore a necklace of crystals. Her piercing green eyes sparkled as if she could see through to the core of everything and everyone.

The woman in simple dress spoke first, "My name is Mary of Magdalene, spouse of Jesus, and this is my daughter, Sarah. We have traveled from a land on the far end of the Great Sea, north of the land of the pyramids, a holy place given to us by God, called Jerusalem."

The other woman in green spoke, "Welcome Mary and," turning to the girl, "welcome Sarah to the land of Avalon. My name is Laudanae, I am a Druid High Priestess, and this is my daughter Venetia. You are welcome to stay here and rest from your journey for as long as you wish. The land of the Druids opens its heart to you, woman of Jerusalem, the land of the Essenes. We have heard much about your land, Moses, David, Solomon and Jesus. The stories of your devotion to God have spread throughout our land."

Venetia reached out her hand to Sarah, "Come let me show you my favorite tree. If you listen with your heart, it will actually talk to you!" "Really, will you show me? I've always wanted to talk to a sacred tree." Sarah laughed with joy. The olive skinned, dark eyed and black-haired Sarah reached out and grasped the hand of her light skinned, green eyed, black-haired new friend. Off they ran toward the forest.

"Venetia and Sarah will talk to the sacred tree to show the union of our two beliefs, you of the Essenes, the belief of the Father, the sacred rites and rituals of the Law of Love and we of the Druids, the way of the Mother, the Earth, the fertility of life, unite here. In this union we complete the Oneness of God here on the Earth, we signify the reflection of the totality of Spirit," Laudanae said bowing her head.

The Magdalene spoke, "Long has it been since these two beliefs were one. I am so glad and my heart is moved that we are here together. Our union will pave the way for generations to come to know we are one in the All."

The Celtic priestess knelt down and placed her hands on a large pumpkin sized shining stone. "Let us infuse our beliefs and honor forever our meeting by touching this stone of quartz and granite. The quartz represents the mystery of God while the granite represents the strength of God. This stone signifies the foundation of life in which we all walk, the solidness of earth that allows the spirit of man to walk and live in this plane. Born eons ago within the earth, the wisdom of the oneness can resides within it. The stone, like a bottomless vase, will hold the memory of the gifts of wisdom we bring here."

The two women knelt next to the stone and placed their hands on it. Closing their eyes, they invoked the power of Spirit to enter into the stone. "Let this stone represent our joining by blessing all who seek the Spirit within and let it bless the earth, sending its peace through the grids of the planet," the Druid priestess said.

They felt a tingling vibration in their bodies. It grew stronger. Their bodies swayed and vibrated in ecstasy. The energy traveled through their arms, then their hands, and left them as it flowed into the stone. The stone hummed, vibrated and from the sky above four rays of light streamed into it.

After moments of silence, absorbing the sacredness of the moment, Laudanae spoke first, "This union of our cultures will not last long. I see legions of shining armor-clad soldiers of Rome marching over our land and taking its riches. Druids will also resist our union as they profess God can only be found within nature. More destruction to our ways will come from other men of Rome, dressed in dark robes and carrying a cross. They will talk about the Messiah and even though they mean well, they will insist that their rules and laws are the only way to find God. After them, I see invasions, wars, plagues, ravishing many lands, cruel people, but I also see devotion, love and many brave souls, growing like flowers through rocky crags."

Mary bowed her head, "This is sad, so very sad. But I see further, much further, two thousand years into the future, I see us returning to a new point in time where everyone will want to know the truth and the ground will be fertile again for a new quest for understanding. Much that we know now will be hidden but then our knowing will return to satisfy the people and lead them to awareness." They held hands over the stone. A wave of soothing profound peace flowed through them.

Laudanae slowly rocked back and forth, "I invoke the peace of our Creator, the Mother and Father God, to radiate out from this Stone, soothing those who seek peace and sanctuary."

A deep sense of peace flowed over Mary, "I, too, invoke this peace and send it into the Stone for others who follow, to use for peace, for he who lives by the sword will die by the sword."

"Come, let us protect this stone and place it in the cave on the side of yonder high hill where it will reside holding the awareness placed in it." Laudanae pointed to a prominent rise of land that stretched upward above the countryside. She then motioned to two men who like sentinels stood behind her. They lifted the stone and followed the two women who, holding hands walked up a twisting path toward the side of the hill.

CHAPTER 1
52 C.E.

After midnight and under the light of a full moon, Roman Centurion Celonius Astarus, commander of an elite Roman cavalry cohort assigned to conquer the Celtic Albion tribes for the Empire, walked through the newly erected compound of brick-walled barracks, stables and workshops. Wearing leather armor, he moved silently through the camp. From the barracks, snores from sleeping men, mumbling from someone dreaming of his lover left long ago in Rome floated through the night. The horses in the corrals and stables stood like silent statues. Off to his left, the training grounds with their mock wood and straw figures cast eerie shadows in the soft quiet light of a full moon.

He walked up a small rise in the center of the camp where a stone building neared completion. This largest structure in the compound would be his command and assembly building. He told his engineers to have its entrance facing east, so that when he entered the building in the morning, Apollo riding his sun chariot, would shine on him. He stood at the entrance, looked out over the surrounding countryside moonlit in silvery white and marveled at the tactical advantage of this new fortress. High on a hill, he and his men could see miles in all directions. Any enemy approaching the fort could be seen long before they could be an actual threat. A few miles to the north, a narrow river ran directly to the sea where precious supplies would arrive for his cohort and the legion.

He couldn't sleep and for the last three nights walked through his fort. Something troubled him deeply. He had served the Empire well, his orders from the commander of Legion II Augusta were clear: subdue and expand. Subdue the Celtic tribes and claim the land now to be called Britannia adding it to the ever-expanding Roman Empire. Subduing the Celts usually meant killing entire families and burning down villages that resisted Roman expansion. The Celts treasured their independence and their mystical nature beliefs. The Celtic Druid priests practiced secret and magical religious ceremonies, which invoked the spirits of the land. They saw the Romans with their controlling governmental rule and their occupational army as a travesty to their way of life and their presence in their land as a sacrilege. The Druids rallied their people to openly oppose the Romans.

In a sort of soft approach, Celonius did not initially seek military action against the Celts. His cavalry would first reconnoiter an area, charge in and demand subjugation to Rome. If the terrified villagers agreed, he moved on and left the main army to occupy and administer the surrounding countryside. If they resisted, he ascertained their strength and fortifications, then attacked if he held an advantage usually with devastating results to the stalwart Celt villagers. Celonius and his men would swoop down like an eagle on a hapless field mouse; the Romans would charge in waves often flanking their opponents, or attacking them from the rear. A master of tactics, Celonius never lost a battle. The cavalry under Celonius rode fast and fought furiously and few Celts could stand up to their shock-and-destroy tactics. Once an area gave in to Roman rule, Celonius and his men moved further west, until they encountered the next group of villages. Ultimatums would be given, Druid resisters were killed and alliances formed. His troop would again continue westward.

To distinguish his unit from all others and to send a message of power to his enemies, all horses in the troop were black. Just the sight of these Romans with their shining armor, red tunics and riding jet-black horses sent terror into those who considered resistance. Many would-be enemies surrendered rather than fight these demons from Rome.

However, the Celts were fierce and courageous, fighting to the last man to protect their villages. When Celonius realized the odds were against him, he waited for the main army to catch up and join him in the attack. His men loved him for his discretion and proved their loyalty in heavy fighting that often ended in dismounted hand-to-hand combat. Tens of thousand of Celts came under Roman rule while Celtic gold and goods flowed into Rome.

The legions highest officer, Vespasian, personally mentioned Celonius to the Emperor Claudius. For his service to the empire, Celonius in an elaborate ceremony had the Emperor's Ring of Gallantry placed on his right forefinger by Claudius himself, the highest honor a Centurion could receive.

With all of his successes, why couldn't he sleep? The local villagers were friendly. In fact, they had welcomed the Romans as they rode into the village. Yet, night after night he walked around his newly constructed fort. He and his men were exhausted and needed rest. With this new fort nearly complete, he hoped he would find peace, a reprieve from the last year of fighting, killing and orders to ride ever westward to expand the empire's frontier.

As he walked toward the fort's perimeter, his sentries, now used to their commander's sleepless nights, saluted. He saluted back but did not talk; his soul too troubled to engage in conversation. He walked up to the sergeant of the night guard dressed in full metal combat armor that reflected the moonlight and appeared to glow. The sergeant snapped to attention at his approach, a sharp quick smack of metal echoed through the still night. Like a silent statue, battle lance straight up and ready, the man did not speak allowing his commander to instigate any conversation.

"Be at ease Titus," Celonius said. He knew military protocol dictated that he call him by rank. Rarely, if ever, did he call a man of the ranks by name, but it was after 2 AM and he had fought side by side with his trusted sergeant for many years. In his longing for sleep and on the night of a warm full moon, Celonius needed companionship not military protocol. "Evening sir," Titus answered still at rigid attention not knowing what to make of his commander's informality.

"Titus I said be at ease, relax," Celonius said. "Thank you sir," Titus' body relaxed and he exhaled a silent sigh of relief. "Beautiful night, sir," Titus said. "Yes, very placid, this whole country side is peaceful. For some reason, I just like it here. Our goddess Terra must love this hill and these trees; she looks out from here and can see forever." "Yes, sir, much nicer here than our last position back east at the river. We did deploy from there quite rapidly; we didn't even complete putting up our barracks and shops. Much talk among the men when that happened," Titus said.

The centurion responded, "I was swimming in the river when the order came to move out; took me by surprise, too. But we're soldiers of Rome and ride when ordered to. We're better off here; we have a commanding view for miles around. Thanks to that river north of here, our cohort and the legion can be re-supplied by ships." But Celonius didn't want to talk about troops and positions, not now; he needed to be with the peace that now seemed to softly touch his soul. "You know Titus, I don't even miss Rome," Celonius said. "People are friendlier here, quite unusual for Celts, they almost were happy to see us. Greeted us even, remember what it was like when we rode in?"

Titus, a seasoned soldier, understood his commander's change of subject, and smiled, "Sir, if I may, you should have seen the look on your face when the daughter of the village elder placed that wreath of flowers on your head."

"By the gods, was it that obvious?" Celonius said, and then laughed. "Oh, yes, here I am demanding them to swear allegiance to the emperor. They smile and this beautiful woman, a Celtic priestess no less, comes and puts flowers around my helmet." Celonius paused to recollect those events a few weeks back while Titus rocked a little on his feet and smiled even more broadly as he, too, remembered their entry into the village a mile or so to the south.

"Did you see how happy they were to see us? If we marched back into Rome we wouldn't have received such a greeting, strange, so strange," the centurion said as he shook his head in disbelief. "Men loved it sir, never seen them this way," Titus replied. "They like it here from what I can see." Celonius said. "Never seen anything like it, sir. No soldier talk here," Titus said. "Soldier talk?" Celonius turned an inquiring glance at his sergeant. "Yes, sir, you know, soldiers aren't happy unless they're complaining. Haven't heard one complaint since we've been here. Not one! Damnedest thing, sir, men are actually joking around and laughing at times," Titus said. "Commander, I've served the emperor for nearly fifteen years, fought all over the empire, I've never seen men act so complacent, like young boys in their mother's lap."

The Centurion's mind snapped back into its military mode of analysis and attack. "This could be dangerous for us," an urgent sense of alarm built up within Celonius. "By the gods, these people could be casting a spell over us. Make us content, happy, and lose our fighting edge. Could we be falling into a trap?"

"Should we double the guard sir?" Titus also jolted from this rapid change of the conversation from light banter to possible threat. He looked at his commander now in deep thought with furrows of concern on his brow, "If this is so sir, then we should be prepared for an attack!"

Celonius pondered the possibility of a sneak attack and then waved his hand dismissing any alarm. Feeling apologetic for violating the peaceful night with his anxiety, "No, No, our daily patrols found no sign of enemy activity anywhere. Searches of the village found only a few weapons. No, I think we're fine." He looked out onto the pastureland below him serenely glowing in the full moon light. He felt a pull to walk out there; his soul yearned to be free from the soldier's life and to walk in peace seeing the beauty of nature without planning the next campaign or defensive position.

"Let me think about this some more. I'm going for a walk out there. The gods seem to be calling me." He stepped forward as a power he had never felt before, a joy in just being alive, flowed over him like a gentle rain on dry parched ground. "Sir, I will call a guard to escort you," Titus said as he snapped back to attention. "No, I'll be fine," Celonius replied, only slightly paying attention to his sergeant. The allure of the night pulled at his heart.

"Sir, you are the commander, regulations state that ..." Titus never finished his protest. Celonius rested his right hand on Titus' shoulder and pressed firmly.

"It's ok Titus, I know all to well what the regulations demand but I have my gladius and I use it well. I'll be fine, I'll be back shortly." The sergeant relaxed, "As you wish Commander. Just call if you need help."

The hill to the south of the encampment although illuminated proved difficult to descend. He carefully climbed down a good distance toward the road that led from the other side of the fort to the meadows below. He could see how it twisted and curved frequently to avoid gullies and streams. He slid down to a bush, which stood on a ledge six feet above the road. He started to grab the bush and use it as a brace to lower himself to the roadbed when he saw them. The two hooded figures walking up the road below caught him by surprise. Their robes glistened in the moonlight, which gave him enough warning to stay hidden behind the bush. With their heads down as if they were in a reverent procession, the approaching figures didn't see the crouched figure above them.

Celonius scanned down the path and saw no one following them. The odds, two to one, were against him, but he held the element of surprise. He had to act quickly; they could be scouts probing his defenses at night looking for weakness. His muscles tensed, the rush of approaching combat sharpened his senses, he waited for them to pass below him then he made his move. Like an eagle diving on its prey, Celonius jumped from the ledge onto the two figures stretching his arms and grabbing each by a shoulder. Using his falling momentum, he pulled them both down hard to the ground. All three fell in a pile, Celonius rolled over, jumped up and pulled out his gladius sword. One of the figures, as fast as Celonius, sprang to his feet and pulled out a Celtic short sword. His hood fell back and Celonius saw the blazing blue eyes and blond hair of a boy who pointed his sword at the Roman ready to fight. Instinctively, Celonius swung his sword knocking the weapon from the youngster. He grabbed the boy by his robe and pulled him forward while raising his gladius up to the youngster throat; the boy froze as a look of terror overcame him.

"No! Please! Please don't hurt him," a woman stood up pulling back her hood. Fear and apprehension filled her eyes. She pleaded again, "Please sir, he's only a boy; don't hurt my brother!" Celonius looked at her while still pressing his sword at the boy's neck. He recognized her as the priestess woman who placed the flowers on his helmet when they entered the village of Bryne. "We mean no harm; we were just out for a walk, tending our flocks, please don't hurt him. He's my young brother, he's only a boy, please, sir." Her voiced strained with fear and passion; she extended her arms to plead with Celonius.

The Centurion looked at her and even in the moonlight covered with a flowing robe, saw her elegance, fairness and beauty. Trained and experienced in analyzing a situation in an instant, he knew these people posed no threat. He lowered his sword but only slightly, his soldier's instincts taking control. 'They could be spies, probing for a weakness in our defenses for a future night attack; after all we are still in unsecured territory. The Legion is not yet present,' he thought; his quick mind debated between his feelings of their seeming innocence and the logic of military analysis.

The woman spoke in a soft reassuring voice, "We are not spies probing for a weakness in your camp. Please relax and be at peace." His head snapped in her direction in amazement at her apparent reading of his thoughts. "What did you say?" he asked. "Sir please, we are no threat to you or your men," she said. Her eyes sparkled in the moonlight enchanting the centurion. Celonius felt an ease come over him and a hint of the peace he had so wonderfully felt when he left the top of the hill.

'A beautiful woman and her younger brother, no threat here,' the Centurion thought. His attitude changed willingly and happily to one of a host greeting visitors to his camp. "Well now, good evening," he said as he lowered his sword to his side. "Go ahead young man, pick up your sword and next time learn how to use it." He paused and looked at both of them closer. The woman riveted his attention. Her long black hair, dazzling green eyes, fair skin, and from what he could tell, slender but firm body as tall as his radiated a beauty and power like the statue of the goddess Juno.

"Dangerous you two walking this close to a Roman garrison at night, my guards don't take prisoners," he said. As the young man with shaking and somewhat shameful hands placed his sword back in his belt, Celonius slid his gladius back in its scabbard. He slid it hard so it made that distinctive snap of metal striking metal, his silent way of announcing his power was still there and ready to be used.

The woman stepped forward and bowed, "Centurion, thank you for your mercy in sparing us, I am Venetia, priestess of the village beyond the pasture land below." The boy quickly stood by her and bowed in succession, "And I, Finian, son of Brandon, thank you too Centurion." Celonius detected a trace of resentment in the boy's voice probably embarrassed by being so rapidly disarmed in front of his sister but his actions were genuine and sincere.

Celonius moved by their openness felt that human part of him awaken. This awakening overshadowed the warrior, the cavalry cohort commander, a centurion of Legion II Augusta, the destroyer of villages and that military mind of analyzing threats and avenues of attack. Like a newly lit candle flickering in a dark room growing brighter until the room softly glowed, his heart felt a warm glow. A feeling he remembered from the distant past as a child in Rome when he sat on his mother's knee and listened to stories about the gods.

"You are a long way from your flocks; they are in the fields below, why are you here?" Celonius asked. Venetia stood in front of him and peered into his eyes. Celonius felt her gaze flow through him like a warm morning breeze moving the cold logic of his military mind. He never had time to love a woman as his duties never permitted it. He felt his desire grow physically as he as a conquering Roman Centurion could take her with or without her consent.

Ever sensitive to those around her, Venetia sensed the desire building within this handsome soldier. She put her right hand up as if sending him a blessing and immediately his lust transformed. Unspoken volumes flowed from eye to eye. Like a Phoenix arising from the ashes, a joy rose within him, a joy and a peace he had never known before. Finian now walked up and put his hand on Celonius' shoulder. "Welcome Centurion. Do you want to follow my sister, Priestess Venetia?"

Venetia whispered, "Come, follow us, can you feel the call in your heart?" "Yes," Celonius said, "that's why I couldn't sleep for the past days. Yes, I can feel it is, it is beautiful." Gone was the power and strength of the Roman Cavalry, replaced with an inner peace, joy, and compassion for these fellow human beings.

"Follow us," Venetia said and together the two robed villagers and the Roman officer walked up the path into a small cave-like opening at the side of the hill. Like a man lost in a hot desert suddenly finding a cool oasis, he bathed in this sublime ecstasy he felt within, which grew stronger as they approached the cave.

CHAPTER 2
408 CE

The remnants of the Roman fort still smoldered. Black smoke blown by the ever-present east wind swirled across the hills hiding the sloping fields and trees like dark clouds eclipsing the sun before a storm. The Roman troops marching far to the east shimmered in the dancing sunlight as their armor reflected the light of the setting sun. The end had come for Rome in Britannia and their dying empire called them back to protect the home land as a mother calls her children home before darkness falls. For some strange reason the Romans never did find the small cave in the hill below their southern defense wall. For almost four hundred years, the cave went unnoticed except in the stories of sacred folklore of the nearby villagers.

The village priests and priestesses had kept the cave hidden and sacred. Only the village elders were allowed to visit their treasure deep within. The cave, not the product of erosion or earth movement, had smooth walls. A descending footpath led toward the cave, which extended into the heart of the hill. In the cave lay the treasure, a treasure of exquisite shape, a treasure of profound importance, a treasure that could not be measured in terms of money but of its impact onto those who could feel its radiant sublime feeling of peace.

Even before the Romans left, the Christian missionaries came and spoke of the Christian God and Jesus who had saved mankind nearly four hundred years before. They set up their church on the hill where the Roman army had built their fort centuries ago. Some of the bricks, cut rocks and concrete slabs were used for the foundation. Their leader, a priest affectionately called Brother Leonidas, went against tradition in building this church to worship Jesus on the ruins of a pagan military outpost.

Brother Leonidas told his fellow missionaries who were placed in his charge, "A church on this hill will be seen for miles around. The cross of Christ sitting on the roof of our church will bless the countryside. All will see it and come to be saved. And look, the front door of the main building faces to the east. I shall make it our church. When we enter in the morning, the sun will shine on us as it did on the tomb of our Master on Easter morning."

Brother Leonidas stumbled on the cave entrance while he was walking the fields meditating on the crucifixion and resurrection of Jesus when he sat down on the side of the hill near the cave entrance. An unusually hot day for England, he felt a cool beckoning breeze touch the back of his neck. As he slowly turned his head to see the source of this mysterious cool air, a fragrant breeze flowed over his face.

'My Jesus is blessing me,' he thought. His heart filled with rapture as he stood up and walked into the soft breeze. Slowly at first, then faster, the breeze created an invisible pathway toward the mouth of the cave. After climbing up the slope, he peered past some low juniper bushes. It was then he saw the cave entrance. "A cave like this was the birthplace of our Master," he thought. He reverently approached the cave, stopped at its entrance, knelt down in great humility and began to pray. At first, with head lowered, he placed his hands together in the traditional prayer position, but as he become more enraptured, he knelt with his body erect and arms outstretched portraying Jesus dying on the cross.

His reverence saved his life. For a Celtic priest, who posed as a sheppard in the field below guarded the cave and took an oath to kill any intruder. When he observed the Christian approaching the cave, the sheppard moved quickly and silently up the hill with his dagger drawn. He silently approached the junipers and turned toward the cave entrance. Wraith like, he crept up behind the kneeling brother. When he saw the Christian kneeling with arms outstretched, he lowered his knife. Brother Leonidas turned to the priest with tears running down his face. The Christian in total rapture made direct eye contact with the Celtic priest. An instant bond developed; the priest knew that this was a holy man he was about to kill. He knew the Christian now touched by the treasure that lay within would never be the same again. They became brothers of the Stone.

The Celt, a learned man named Geflin, spoke Latin; he smiled at the short statured stranger. The two men spoke slowly and carefully, both knowing their cultures and backgrounds like two mountains separated by a long and treacherous valley were miles apart. However, the cave bound them together. Leonidas experienced a warm glowing sensation in his heart. "It's Jesus, I feel him in my heart. He's speaking to me."

"This cave has been here for many years. By Roman count of time, hundreds of years," Geflin said. "The holy ones left it here. Our ancestors have told us that strangers from a far land, a holy women and a child, came and talked with our high priestess. Together they blessed this cave and made it sacred. It's the home of our treasure. We have kept it hidden from the Romans." Leonidas asked, "What's inside? Surely, it must be something from God and His angels. It has been said the mother of our savior, his wife and child had come to Britannia, but I never thought it was true."

The Celtic priest stood up and like a fully-grown oak tree his majesty and countenance overshadowed everything around him. He pulled at the tie rope that held his tunic at the neck and the brown tattered garment fell to the ground. The radiance that came from the priestly robe shown like a beacon in the darkened cave entrance. His robe, the color of ivory, made his beard and long dark hair look like shiny coal atop a mound of virgin snow.

"Follow me," said Geflin, "and I will show you our treasure, for you have been touched by it as I can see in your eyes and heart. This is providential for the energy of our treasure is dying and we fear it will be lost forever. The spirits who are hidden from your view but not mine, are beckoning you forward. You are now one of us." "But I'm a follower of Jesus, the Son of God. It is God or his angels that I must be feeling. It is so beautiful," Leonidas said.

"Then your God or Angels are the same as ours. For you see, I have been touched like my father before me. Look into my eyes," Geflin said. Leonidas arose and stood in front of the priest. The Brother, smaller than the other man and somewhat heavy for his height, stood firmly with a masculine strength and firmness. He stared into the Celtic's eyes. He saw a deep compassion that instinct told him could only come from a man who has seen God. "Come my brother," Leonidas said, "show me your treasure." The two men turned and walked into the cave.

CHAPTER 3
Two Years Ago

I arrived at Heathrow Airport in London and dodged through crowds of other travelers, most of them dragging their luggage. There were thousands of people walking in front of me in the concourse and hindering my progress. The PA system echoed throughout the terminal announcing arriving and departing flights. People from all over were talking, sometimes quite loudly so they could be heard over the constant growing noise. Being from New York and accustomed to crowds, I plodded onward toward a group of men holding greeting signs with their travelers' names. One of the University's aides was to meet me and take me to my first archeological dig in England. And there he was, a well-dressed man stood with a sign that said 'Elliot Rizzo'. I felt relief at seeing my name in this hectic airport.

To my surprise my greeter wasn't to drive me to the dig site. The polite gentleman from the University handed me a brochure on what trains and buses to take to get close to the dig site, where upon my arrival in the small town of Horningsham, I was to call the local cab company for a ride to the site. Being a young twenty four-year old graduate archeology student from the US on my first major UK dig, and after hearing horror stories from fellow students about walking for days through a desert or bouncing on a camel to get to their first dig site, I realized I shouldn't have expected better treatment.

Two train rides and one pleasant bus ride brought me to the town a mile from the dig site. Sitting in the bouncing bus, I gazed out the window at the English country side with its rolling hills, farm lands and stands of trees, so unlike the concrete and steel buildings of busy New York. This brought me a peaceful drifting feeling returning my thoughts to the events in my teenage years that led me to this moment in my life. I thought back to the burning fascination I had with the Roman Empire. How the Romans expanded their rule around the world and, most fascinating of all, their four century long occupation of Britannia, what is referred to as present day England.

As a youngster, I remember checking out an old library book that had a picture of a Roman Centurion on a black horse. I stared at the young warrior, his glistening armor, red crested helmet and red riding cloak, holding a shining gladius sword out in front of his rearing horse and leading his soldiers to attack. I carefully cut the page out of the book, close to the binding, with one of my father's razor blades. My work, artful and precise, showed no sign of the missing page. Mrs. Weber, our stern-faced, heavy rimmed glasses-wearing librarian, who could catch the slightest microbe of a pencil mark upon a return book, never discovered my sinister plot. I taped the picture of the Centurion over my bed, hoping one day I would be like this brave dashing Roman warrior.

The squealing of the bus's brakes snapped me back to the present; we had reached our destination. The massive clock on the side of the building in this small town read 2pm. We had arrived at the small old hotel that was a dormitory for the dig team. Lugging my bags, I walked to the front desk to check in and a short elderly heavyset woman with a roundish likeable face said, "Ah, yes, you're the Yank they've told me about. Here's the key to your room, B11, you're sharing it with a wonderful fellow from Germany who is also a student. I'll call a taxi and have them drive you to the site," she said smiling with a naturally jovial manner. "Far from here?" I asked. "Oh, not far, you'll be there shortly."

Thirty minutes later, sitting in the back of the taxi, I again admired the peaceful rolling hills of the English countryside. The narrow road curved through the green and brown farmland. Part of me felt calm and relaxed, hypnotized by the pattern of the ever flowing green fields. Another part of me felt anxious and jumpy, like a racehorse at a starting gate. The cab driver, an older gentlemen wearing a plaid shirt and speaking with a heavy English accent, acted as my tour guide. He pointed to each farmhouse and told me who lived there with a short biography of each family.

Finally, the dig site came into view. So did a burst of mixed emotions. They flowed over me like Old Faithful sprouting a giant plume. On the one hand, I felt elation at being able to delve into my passion of archeology. On the other hand, I would be 'the new kid on the street' trying to be one of the guys and I felt a bit apprehensive in meeting new people from different countries. Far from my campus and big city, I was the proverbial "fish out of water." Previously I had some annoying experiences with groups and knew how cliquish they could be. But this was not to happen; in fact it was just the opposite.

The view of the site that greeted me when I got out of the cab is burned in my mind to this day. The student diggers worked diligently with trowels and brushes, some standing in small groups intently discussing what appeared to be an artifact they had uncovered; some students lay on the ground, or knelt, brushing away the dark brown dirt from an ancient square block that looked like part of a wall. I didn't notice Professor Charles Weldon smiling at me as I stood there. My attention was immediately fixed on an attractive woman, a student I presumed, who knelt on all fours, brushing fine dust from a piece of grey pottery. With delicate hands she pushed back her long brown hair that laced over her shoulders. I didn't even notice Dr. Weldon as he walked towards me hand outstretched in greeting, his eyes followed my gaze.

"Yes, very nice scenery here, I'm Dr. Charles Weldon, and you are Elliot Rizzo, ah, from New York, yes?" He said while walking towards me conscious of my rapt attention elsewhere.

I immediately snapped out of my trance and jumped at his jovial greeting. "Yes, yes, thank you Dr. Weldon," I stuttered out, "I'm really looking forward to working with you." I felt somewhat embarrassed by being caught looking at this attractive woman and not introducing myself immediately to my dig professor and future mentor. When our eyes connected, I felt I had known Dr. Weldon before, a déjà vu sensation, that "Where do I know you from?" feeling that most of us have experienced at one time or another. For this reason and for others that will be unveiled later in my story, I will refer to him as Charles.

Charles smiled, "Yes, yes, let me introduce you to the team. We'll be working hard together for the next few weeks." "Miss Phillips," Charles said as we walked over to the attractive young woman, "this is Elliot Rizzo, one of your countryman, here to help find the lost Roman Legion." I overlooked Charles' reference to a lost Roman Legion as Miss Phillips stood up and said, "Hi, Ann, UCLA." She put out her hand and we shook, "Elliot, NYU."

Her eyes shone a deep blue and her countenance overwhelmed me. Her smile and bounciness resonated through me and uplifted me. Totally disarmed from my ego defenses, I felt empowered by her presence. "Have you found the Holy Grail yet?" I asked in a feeble attempt at humor to impress her.

Charles snapped immediately, "No, but maybe we'll find it tomorrow," as he held my left shoulder tightly and turned me toward the rest of the team who were performing all sorts of jobs at the site. He walked me to each one introducing me as the new team member. He did this with a certain friendliness that instilled a sense of camaraderie in me. Charles, a natural leader, had from what I immediately sensed changed a group of foreign students into a well-organized team within the few days they had been working together.

CHAPTER 4
My First Dig

For the rest of the day, I worked along with Kurt from Germany who would be my roommate at the hotel. We slowly dug following the outline of a wall trying to establish its length and direction. My Master Thesis focused on Roman construction techniques so clearing this wall not only interested me but also allowed me to offer some insight into how it might have been built. Every now and then I turned to watch Ann. Was it coincidence that when I turned, she seemed to be looking at me also?

As my first week progressed, I found Ann fun to talk to. She listened to me when I jabbered on about the importance of archeology and how it opened up gateways to the past. In fact, she hung onto my every word. This made me feel so good, so important. Ann also treated me as no woman ever did before. Listening intently to what I said, agreeing with my ideas, asking questions when she didn't quite 'get it' and politely disagreeing or prodding me to see another point of view when her views differed from mine. In turn, I out of sense of mutual respect acted the same with her. Our mutual attraction and respect, I had to say, made me feel quite masculine and self-assured.

But I digress, back to my first day. As the sun set, we covered up the site with tarps. A bus took us back to the hotel and after a quick shower and fresh clothes, we all gathered in the hotel's small dining room for supper and a talk about the day's finds. We joked and laughed in those few hours after supper before we went to bed. However, at the dig site, everything was professinal. Charles ran a business-like operation, giving each of us, defined tasks and rewarding us with praise when we completed them. For example, Kurt and I uncovered a wall by digging six inches deep and six feet along its length each day. Charles came over every hour or so, inspected our work and showed us features that confirmed the purpose of the wall.

"See these rusted iron nails at the top of the wall? They held objects just like leather bridles or some sort of tools or weapons," Charles said. "But this is a small outside wall, only six feet long, obviously part of a building, hut or house. We need to find the other walls connected to it in order to find the inside of the main structure". He stood over the wall's east end, facing north. "Tomorrow, from this end, lay out your dig line in this direction," he pointed to the north. "The inside of the structure is probably on the north side of the wall. We're standing at the outside of the wall now."

Some of the other team diggers came over to listen to Charles's description of the building. Kurt walked over and paced out the path where Charles had pointed. "Here, to the left of the wall we've uncovered?" Kurt asked." Yes, good," said Charles. But, as I stood looking at them, I just knew they were wrong. An almost irresistible urge came over me to say 'No, its this way, to the south, to the right of the wall, we are inside the structure now. This is the inside of the wall not the outside.' Call it intuition, a sixth sense, or whatever, but I just knew the structure was to the right of the wall, not the left. I could see it, almost vision-like, a small hut like building, a guard building for a sentry suddenly appeared in my mind's eye. Like a present day military installation, the front gate always has a guard or gatehouse for sentries or military police. I just knew, I could see it, almost like a memory.

Somewhat bewildered by what I had just experienced, I felt dizzy and sat down on the ground next to our excavation, lowered my head and started to take in deep breaths to get more oxygen in my system. I felt Ann next to me, sitting on my right, even though I didn't look up, I could feel and sense her presence.

Her knee brushed up against mine, "You OK, New York?" "Yeah, I'm good, but I just had this real weird feeling", I answered. "Maybe its my perfume, I bought it to entrap you," Ann said, brushing my knee again, this time, to my delight, her knee touched mine and she left it there, firmly. It's amazing how a simple touch can relay volumes.

I laughed, "You don't need perfume to do that." "So what's bugging you?" she asked. I told Ann of my intuition and vision. "But how do I tell that to Charles? 'Errrr, Sir, excuse me but you're wrong, I just had a feeling we should dig in another direction.'" Ann snuggled up closer to me and spoke softly, "Why don't you just make a suggestion, that to save time and explore all options, ask if you could dig on the other side of the wall just in case the building might be inside the wall and not outside?" I reached across with my left hand and touched Ann. "Thanks, have you ever thought about giving up archeology and getting into public relations?" "Maybe, maybe I'll do both. So are you just going to sit here?" Ann said.

I walked over to Kurt and Charles and explained my alternative approach pretty much the way Ann had worded it. Puffing on his pipe, Charles looked at me for an agonizingly long minute. Finally he said, "Hmmmm, I like your idea, Elliot, shows insight and efficiency. Lord knows we are short of time and money." After a few more puffs, he raised his clipboard and started to write while he announced, "Tomorrow, Kurt, you dig the way I suggested and, Elliot, you dig like you have suggested." He walked to the west end of the wall, and pointed south, "Over here, set up your dig line... here, to the south." I walked over to Charles to get a good look at where he pointed. It turned out to be exactly where my vision had seen the rest of the structure. He laughed put his hand on my shoulder, "let's hope your idea is correct and all your work doesn't 'go south' as you Yanks are fond of saying." "Thank you Professor Weldon, I'm sure it won't," I said. I looked at Ann and winked, we both smiled. 'Life is wonderful,' I thought. It would soon turn out to be better than I could ever imagine.

The next day, I uncovered the second wall exactly where my intuition said it would be. "How did you know that?" Kurt asked at that evening's supper. "Don't know, lucky guess," I answered. Ann, sitting next to me, leaned over and gently whispered in my ear, "It's because you're smart." I blushed and felt her admiration.

Similar sensations came from other conversations with Ann, which lasted past our curfew. Charles wanted us in bed by 10:30pm so we would have fresh minds for the morning dig. Ann and I talked about Rome, archeology, school, our parents, our lives and our futures. The talks started with us sitting in the lounge of the hotel. A day or two later we took a walk, slowly bumping into each other, our primal way of touching. Then we graduated to arm in arm and within a week we were kissing, softly at first and growing more passionately.

We were both happy and starting to fall in love with each other. But we didn't let our feelings and admiration for each other affect our work at the dig site. In fact, we became more enthusiastic and worked harder as some mysterious emotion within both of us was fulfilled by our mutual affection. Charles aware of our growing relationship remained distant, observing that our work at the site met his expectations of how graduate students should perform.

Although old enough to be my father, Charles and I quickly developed a deep friendship. We joked often and became the camp comedians to the joy and laughter of the rest of the team. Our interest in old England, the Roman occupation and early Christianity led to many open discussions, which drew in the rest of our team.

CHAPTER 5
The First Vision

Here we were, two graduate students in our second week away from home and overwhelmed with a myriad of emotions and experiences. One night, Ann and I strolled through a well-lit town park not far from our hotel; we found such comfort and joy in being together. The park was quiet, with a small brook sheltered by trees, cut lawns on slowly rising ground; it had all the makings of a romantic hideout for us. I imagined during the day, hordes of people would descend on such a sacred spot dotting the grounds with picnickers, frisbee games, dog walkers and young mothers with their baby carriages. But tonight, with just a few couples like us either strolling down the paths or sitting close together on benches, the park became a sanctuary.

A stand of large oaks bordered the path we walked. I put my hand in hers and she held it tighter than a casual squeeze. "We've been on our feet all day, let's sit for awhile," Ann said. "Under this great oak, away from the path," I said as I gently pulled her toward the inviting tree trunk that curved perfectly with a chair like impression big enough for both of us. We sat down and were quiet for a few moments just enjoying that electric feeling that flowed between us. "Ann, I like the way I feel when I'm with you. I like the way I've changed since I met you," I said. I held her hand tighter, feeling my love for her swelling inside of me.

"That's wonderful to hear Elliot. You've changed me too. You don't argue with me or try to prove you're better. So many guys I met try to do that but I feel so comfortable with you. This is rare for me and I thank you." She rested her head on my shoulder and exhaled deeply. I placed my arm around her. The warmth of being so close sent a soothing tingle through me. "Oh Ann, this feels so good," I whispered, my face resting in the softness and sweet fragrance of her brown silky hair. "Yes it does Elliot," she whispered, as lovers do, we turned to each other and kissed, deeply and softly.

"I feel so wonderful but so tired; I'm not used to all of this physical work," her voice softened and seductively tapering off into a murmur. She burrowed her head deeper into my chest. Within seconds, she fell asleep. I held her closer, shut my eyes and, after the rigors of digging all day in the heat of the English farmlands, carting wheelbarrows of dirt, and inspecting minute fragments of ancient scraps, while leaning up against an old oak tree with Ann snuggled up next to me, her breath falling into a soft feminine cadence, I fell into a deep sleep.

What happened next is difficult to describe but I'll give it a try. I started spinning or spiraling in a clockwise direction. A droning vibration and noise like a heavy rain shower accompanied the spiraling and, within a few seconds, I started to panic. I had never experienced anything like this; even getting drunk at a frat party didn't come close to this spinning sensation. After a few moments, it slowly subsided and I became aware of myself in a very vivid dream or vision. I felt alive, real and became aware of observing myself in a different place and at a different time.

I walked down to a narrow river and took off my clothes to go for a swim. But they weren't clothes like I wear today; I recognized them immediately as Roman soldier garb, the half tunic, leather armor, sandal leggings and a short gladius sword on a finely fitted leather belt around my waist. Even as an observer, I perspired from the heat. I felt the muscles in my body and as I took off my sandals and waded into the stream, I felt the rocks of the riverbed pressing into my bare feet.

Then my point of reference changed dramatically. I'm no longer the observer; I'm really there. This is me; I am walking into the river, for real. The water felt cool over my hot body; I waded out into the stream deeper, up to my waist. Oh, how cool the water felt and I wanted more of it. I stretched my arms forward and plunged into the cooling waters. Immediately the river absorbed the heat of my body, replacing the hot tired muscles ache with a cool invigorating chill. I lay motionless underwater, relaxing in this soothing loving liquid. I kicked up to the top, took a few strokes and rolled over on my back. I laid face up in the cool river looking up at puffy white clouds and a bright blue sky. I took in a gulp of water, spit it out in a long stream. I let out a yell, a deep bellow of satisfaction and, to my surprise, with power and gusto, a deep baritone escaped me.

Now standing chest high, I raised my arms, shook the water off of my hair that I could sense was thick and long. I looked at my arms and saw smooth developed muscles. A bronze like metal band wrapped around my left wrist and a large silver ring with an embossed Roman Eagle rested securely on my right forefinger. My skin, dark with sun exposure, glistened through droplets of water. I never felt so strong, powerful, determined, confident, alert and at ease.

I looked at the shore; an odd shaped hill with a camel like double hump silhouetted the horizon. Just below the hill, between it and the stream, stood a stone fort-like structure on an open plain. Some of its buildings seemed incomplete, their walls with scaffolding only a few feet high. A coral with hundreds of black horses at its right; a road to its left seemed to wind back around the hill. I could see men in Roman battle armor engaged in mock sword fights, training for a future engagement.

'An ideal place to position a military outpost,' I thought. 'Plenty of water, only one road through the meadow, sentries can control access in and out. We are secure, protected and, most important, hidden,' Yes, I thought this with the confidence of a battle hardened military commander. Then a stab of dismay brought an unsettled feeling in my stomach, 'But, in the future, we must leave this well-placed fort, turn it over to the occupation troops, and, like so many times before, ride westward.'

A soldier came running to the shore calling to me, disrupting my thoughts, "Commander, an urgent dispatch has been received."

'They can't want us to move out so soon,' I thought. 'What surprise awaits us now?' But I never did find out the contents of the dispatch. I started to walk out of the stream toward the soldier who started talking to me again when a loud buzz shot through my head. I could hear no more, his voice broke up into meaningless jabber and everything started to spin. The sky, the river, the horses, the humped back hill, twirled around me in a swirl of buzzing, jabbering and flying scenery. I spiraled counterclockwise this time as I came to a spinning return to the present.

Then, silence, warmth, the wonderful touch of soft wet lips on my left cheek accompanied with the fragrance of a woman…. I snapped my eyes open, saw trees, a woman kneeling next to me. I shook in panic. I didn't know who or where I was. My thoughts raced; where's the river, my soldiers, the horses? What the hell is going on…. where am I? More importantly, who am I?

"Oh my God, Elliot, what's wrong, did you have a bad dream? You were out like a light," she whispered. Again her wonderfully soft lips kissed me, she hugged me closely. As I starred at her, I wanted to jump, to yell, but pins and needles shot through my body. I put my head down, covered it with my hands, and rocked slowly back and forth trying to orient myself.

Finally, a flood of awareness came; I knew who I was, where I sat and who Ann was. Along with this awakening came a feeling of relief. The panic vanished, the confusion vanished, and, once again, I am Elliot Rizzo, graduate student with a promising exciting career as an archeologist sitting next to an attractive woman who I am starting to fall in love with. Ann sat back frowning with concern. I sat somewhat mesmerized and detached. Like a young mother prodding a reluctant child, Ann said, "Well talk about rejection. Elliot, what's going on, are you sick?"

"I'm ok, I'm ok," I said trying to convince her and myself at the same time. "You're scaring me, like, you're in a trance, like a zombie," she said. Pragmatism came back to me "How do you know what a zombie looks like?" I asked. She poked me in the ribs; it hurt but felt good. "The weirdest thing happened to me," I said and explained the scene and the events I recalled. "So you actually were a Roman soldier, bathing in a river, hmmm," she said.

I could see the polite look of disbelief on her face. "Look its getting late, we've been working hard, immersed in this Roman stuff, anything can happen. Maybe your dream was just a fantasy your mind made up to make sense of it all. Our minds are very complicated." "You don't believe me, do you?" I asked feeling somewhere between lost and annoyed. Lost, searching for an explanation for this scary experience and annoyed, because it was so real and she did not believe me. "Maybe I do and maybe I don't. What matters is that we've got to be back on site early tomorrow morning or

Professor Weldon will have our hides pinned to that Roman wall you and Kurt uncovered. So let's go!"

Ann stood up, grabbed my hand, and with strength that surprised me, pulled me up to my feet. She wrapped her arm around my waist, pulling me along as she walked toward the park exit. "Forget it, Elliot, we both need sleep, curfew time is here, let's go back to the hotel," Ann said. We walked arm in arm, the cooling night and Ann's strength hauled me back down to reality. But I felt betrayed in a way, this vision, this experience, so real to me seemed to be somewhat of an illusion to her. I just wish she would have believed me or taken it more seriously.

But I let the whole incident go and took comfort in Ann's arm around me and mine around her. I dismissed the vision experience, moving it to the back of my mind like putting an old jacket in the corner of a closet not to be used until next winter. Little did I know I would be taking it out and wearing it again the next day.

CHAPTER 6
Down by the River

The next day, drizzle and a damp heavy fog hangs over the valley. A typical morning in central England, greeted our team as we started digging. We had worked for over a week with nominal success by uncovering the remnants of a small structure with a few artifacts. A broken knife, pottery shards and a few pieces of hardware, nails, hinges, hitch rings and so on were carefully recorded in our site log. After we assembled at the site, Charles gathered us in a group and questioned us as to what we found.

Kurt responded, "The remains of the small building suggest it served as a blacksmith or craftsman shop; it may be significant." Thomas, a graduate student from Sheffield University in England said, "a small utility building of some sort." Everyone murmured and muddled over what they thought the building might have been used for and whether we should do anymore work on it.

"A small structure or shack yes, but at least its something," Ann said. Then almost instinctively I blurted out, "It's more than a shack, it's a sentry outpost to a Roman cavalry barracks. Their main camp can't be too far away." I surprised myself as I spoke but couldn't control my words as they just flowed out of me. "Really!" Charles said as the others stopped their chattering to stare at me like a class of geography students just hearing a classmate declare the world is flat after all.

"Yes," I said feeling uncomfortable. "Elliot?" Ann asked with that 'how could you?' look on her face. "In fact," I continued, "if you let me scout around, I could probably find it for you." The team stood in shock and silence. I stood there trying to stand tall and look sure of myself while I hoped that the nervous twitch of my upper lip wouldn't give me away. I relaxed when Charles smiled. He seemed quite amused by my boldness.

"Oh, you Yanks, my God, must you always try to search for or explore something on your own? Our advanced team searched around this entire area and they said this was the likely spot." He pointed to our important but somewhat meager findings, which I think caused an 'Aha moment' for him. He mumbled quietly, 'not much here actually.' "Follow me Mr. Rizzo," Charles said. He walked toward the edge of our site, placed his hands behind him and stared out over the fields. I stood next to him. "So tell me, Elliot, how do you know there's a main camp?" Charles asked. He lowered his voice so no one in our group of students could hear him.

"I had a vision, last night, a dream maybe, Professor Weldon. I mean, it was like I was there, like I'm a Roman soldier, an officer, swimming in a river, I could see the barracks, it was so real." I stammered, "and… I just can't get it out of my mind. I need to look for what I saw, I mean what I experienced in that vision." I closed my eyes, shook my head, 'There I said it,' I thought, 'either he's going to believe me or I'll be a laughingstock this evening.' He silently looked out over the fields and hills. "Ok, very well, go ahead, give it a go," he looked at me and smiled with a look of encouragement and a vague sense of approval, "Go scout around, and if you do find this main post, you get an A+." "Deal," I said as I put out my hand to shake Charles'. "Err… yes, that's American, very well," Charles said as he offered his hand, "Deal."

While my fellow team members starred in disbelief, I walked off toward the hills pausing for a second to grab my backpack and bottled water. The land I walked belonged to a huge farm and the owner had given permission to the University to explore it for anything that had to do with the history of England. I walked for no more than a few minutes realizing that if indeed that small ruin was a building for Roman sentries, the main post had to be within a short distance. I crested a small hill with our dig site in the hollow below, I looked down on the site and could make out the faint depression forming the outline of an ancient road that passed in front of the sentry post through the hollow. 'Yes, it makes sense', I thought, 'anyone traveling up this road would be stopped by the Roman sentries as they checked the traffic in and out of the main post'.

To focus on the direction of the road, I pointed at it and followed it with my hand. It disappeared at times where it blended in with the surrounding land but then it would reappear some meters farther on as a faint outline sunk below grade. I lost it all together behind another hill a few hundred meters further. All the pieces of my vision were fitting together, my body shook in apprehension as I ran down the hill and picked up the old road, which now appeared as a slight dent in the ground. It meandered around the hill then curved through a small pass and finally opened up to a flat plain about a quarter mile long. There before me lay what I was searching for, breathing rapidly in excitement and from running, I jumped up and down and howled raising my fist in the air in a victory salute.

"Yes! Yes!" I screamed. Ten meters in front of me, twisting its way through the far end of the plain, lay a dried out river bed. 'The river in my vision?' I thought. I need to walk it and find the place where I swam and could see the double hump hills, if they were still around and not worn down by erosion. From that point in the river, I should be able to locate the main barracks, stables and buildings I saw in my vision.

I walked along the dried out riverbed which now appeared as a depression ranging from fifty to seventy five feet wide and only a few inches or so deep. A far cry from what I experienced in my vision when I could swim and barely touch the bottom. Two thousand years had changed the landscape. Perhaps, some ancient event changed the flow of the river and the riverbed filled up with blowing dirt and sediment from two millennia of rain and silt.

My walk turned into a trot then a run. My enthusiasm grew as I ran with the plain to my left, the hills behind the plain and the river to my right. I developed a steady trot, anxious to cover the ground and find the hills that looked like a camel hump as soon as I could. Half way through the plain, the riverbed curved to the right. I loosely followed the riverbed staying more toward the plain to its left. This location gave me a better chance to find the elusive camel humped hill.

But, no luck. As I neared the end of the plain with the river now fifty meters or so away, I stopped my trot and stood panting, half from excitement and half from anxiety. No double hump hill. I stood in disbelief. "No!" I said out loud, "it has to be here." It all makes sense. The guard post down the road, the flat plain, the river, the hill has to be here too. The English landscape is stable; two thousand years, is a blink of an eye in geologic times, the hills couldn't have moved that much. Rivers dry up but hills don't move. Or do they? Maybe erosion did wear them away and I would never find that hill.

I sat down and rested, always better to think when my mind is clear and relaxed. I remember from physiology class, 'the higher the Alpha brainwave energy, the clearer the mind.' I sucked in large gulps of air and started to relax. I felt my anxiety slowly drift away. I took a drink of water and deliberately began to analyze why I didn't see the double hump hills.

It came to me in an instant, 'Of course I couldn't find it. In my vision I was in the river not running along it. That difference in height from being in the water below the shore line to my six foot height above it could be enough to throw off the angle of sight and make everything look different.' I picked up a clump of grass in my right hand, pulled it up and threw it down, and congratulated myself for this cool analytical thinking. I had to try again. I got up and walked to the center of the dried up river, then trotted down to the far end. 'Ok, I'll start here and slowly work my way back to the beginning of the river and toward the guard house.'

But as I walked up the riverbed and looked over the hills behind the plain, where the double hump hill should be, after walking the entire length, I still could not find it. The idea that I could be wrong and my vision came from an imaginary dream state started to gnaw away at my enthusiasm. I decided to get lower, to make my eyes on a level with a person who is in the river itself, like in the vision. I trotted again to the far end of the riverbed. I squatted down so my head leveled about two feet above the shoreline. Not exactly the same as the vision but close enough. Then I started the strained journey of duck walking staying in a squat position back up the dried river bed, focusing, remembering my vision on the hill outline to the west, looking for that tell tale double hump hill. I reasoned that in two thousand years the natural layering of dirt, grass and vegetation would have raised the ground level by about ten feet, that's why the riverbed is higher. This natural rise would also change the tops of the hills, which are also subject to erosion by wind and rain.

Keeping all of this in mind, I squatted and walked like a duck, until my legs ached and I had to sit down and rest. I took an energy bar out of my backpack. It tasted good. The midday sun was high and the weather had cleared; now I was in hot humid English summer climate. I took out a water bottle and drank half the water. I needed to stay hydrated; my senses need to stay keen. I felt the sweat pour down my face and body. Ringlets of sweat flowed down my sides and stomach and I could feel my skin stick to my shirt. Off went my jacket, folded and put it away in my backpack.

Refreshed and rested, I took a deep breath and started my duck walk up toward the mouth of the riverbed. Twenty-five feet later I stopped; there they were. Two hills close together, and in my growing more painful squatting position, they looked like a camels hump. When I stood up and looked, there were still two hills in front of me but the change in height as little as it was, made the camel hump harder to discern. No wonder I couldn't see it before.

I quickly calculated the location of the main fort. I closed my eyes and played back my vision. I pretended again to be bathing in the river, my angle in the water and then pointed to where the main buildings were. Opening my eye, my finger pointed to a landscape almost the same as in my vision the night before. I made a mental note of a shrub that stood in line with where I pointed and ran to it. Pain immediately shot through my legs. The toll of walking squatted for the last ten minutes tightened my leg muscles so much, I could hardly walk. I sat down, massaged my legs, I needed to take care of myself.

After what seemed like a lifetime, I stood up and felt the bounce come back to my legs and the 'thrill of the hunt' made me sprint like a lion chasing its prey. Full of excitement, I got to the shrub and looked around for any sign of a wall, a roof or any geometrical pattern in the ground that would indicate a substructure. I had to bring back something to Charles; I needed some sort of proof. I looked around and saw nothing but grass, shrubs and dirt. 'It has to be here. Start looking, do a search pattern, walk in larger concentric circles around this point,' I thought. Still unable to quite control myself, I started running in my search pattern, looking around for any sign of a structure hidden in the ground.

I didn't find it; it found me! As I started my third circle out from the shrub, my left foot stubbed on something solid, l stumbled, falling forward, my pack made me top heavy enough to lose my balance, I hit the ground face down.

CHAPTER 7
My Dream Comes True

Laying face down, I pulled my hands up to my chest and did a push up to right myself. I rolled to my left and looked down at my left foot, which was starting to hurt from smashing into whatever I had tripped over. Looking past my foot, sticking out of the ground stood what I had been looking for: a dull red flat brick, but not any brick, by its square flat thin size I beheld an ancient brick, a building block made two thousand years ago by the Romans, an artifact indicating they were here. I threw archeological procedures to the wind, no mapping or sketching on how it lay in the ground, and pried it from the ground. I quickly examined it. At a foot square and two inches thick and tile like, I had no doubt I held a Roman brick. I scanned the area for more clues but saw nothing of a building or ruins, just dirt and grass field. But I held the proof I needed, a Roman sized brick, right where it should be as in my dream.

I trotted back toward the dig site, backpack and gear bobbing and sweat running down my body in the midday sun. I examined the brick closely while trotting and realized

I couldn't have asked for a better artifact. Unlike a modern day brick used for walls, the Roman brick, flatter and thinner, could be used to build a wall, or be used as a floor or roof tile. To my delight, remnants of cement or mortar adhered to one side of the brick, enough to show that this brick belonged to a larger structure. Perhaps from one of the buildings I saw in my vision.

I crossed over the sunken road to the field where my coworkers were excavating. On their knees trowling and brushing away dirt, they resembled a group of artisans at their craft rather than archeologists searching for clues of the past. Charles, their overseer stood with his clipboard diligently directing them. "I found it, I found it!" I yelled as I drew closer. I felt like Paul Revere racing through the night awakening sleeping colonists. My colleagues stopped and looked up at me. I gulped with nervousness as Charles put his clipboard under his arm and approached me. I expected to be met with skepticism and a scolding for not following archeological protocol by unceremoniously prying the brick from the ground without officially recording its place in a site map.

Instead, the whole team, with Charles in the lead greeted me like a soldier coming home from the war. I guess they all sensed the drudgery of working on this small hut knowing that a richer and larger prize awaited them somewhere nearby. And I had found what they were waiting for.

"Look, a brick, part of a wall, the whole fort has to be up there!", I said as I stopped, bending over, panting to catch my breath and pointing in the general direction of the flat plain. When Charles stood in front of me, I stood erect like a marine in front of a drill sergeant and handed my trophy over to him. His eyes lit up the moment I placed it in his hands. Chatter, back pats, handshakes followed, but what I liked the most came from Ann. She looked deep into my eyes, "I knew you could do it." She kissed me on the cheek, quickly, professionally so as to not reveal our mutual feelings to the team, but the electricity of her touch sent a thrill through me. I blushed.

After examining the brick with his magnifying glass Charles said, "Definitely Roman, look here at these letters." Everyone shuffled in to get a look, He read aloud "L-E-G-I-O", paused for a second, then read "I-I". You see, the Roman Legions carried kilns so they could cast and bake bricks to build their structures. Each legion would imprint their name on their bricks." Holding up the brick, "we have here a brick made by Legion II Augusta who marched through here anywhere from 46 to 52 CE." Every one cheered and I received another volley of back pats and handshakes.

"Elliot, can you take me to where you found this wonderful artifact?" "Right this way," I said as I waved my hand toward the plain. "The rest of you keep working at your assigned tasks," Charles said as he pointed to the sentry outpost. "We'll be back directly." As we walked toward the plain, my stomach started to feel queasy. 'Did I do something wrong? Maybe I should have left the brick in its place? What if there isn't anything else there? What if it's just a brick that somebody scavenged and used it in some old broken down farmhouse? What if my vision was only a dream and not real at all?' My mind raced with these questions.

Charles, never in a rush, took on a big brother manner and gently but firmly asked me to explain again how I knew where to look. He remained quiet during my explanation of my vision and then asked how I found a few tell-tale signs like the dried up riverbed and the double hump hills. We walked as a teacher and student through the plain. He the teacher guiding the conversation flow and I, the student, talking quickly using hand gestures to add emphasis to key points. We walked the grounds on the plain where I found my trophy brick but could not identify much detail. Charles, with his experience in surveying a potential site, suggested we climb one of the hills to the west for a better view of the plain.

He was right. We crested a hill that stood about 20 meters or more above the plain below and looked down from a different perspective. "See here, my young American cowboy," he pointed toward the center of the plain where I found the brick, "tell me what your eyes tell you." I followed his pointing finger.

"Yes, yes," I said, "I see it!" Charles smiled as a pattern of depressions in the ground revealed a grid of intersecting lines that could be the outline of buildings buried under the ground. The patterns covered hundreds of square yards comprising at least four or five large size structures.

"Yes, yes," I exclaimed as I jumped and waved my fist in the air. The vision, the double hump hill, the river, everything came together and made sense. But most of all, my diligence in surveying the land and perseverance in duck walking up and down the riverbed created a deep sense of accomplishment. Charles patted me on the back, "Congratulations, Elliot, you get an A+ for this course and writing your thesis on what we find here will land you your doctorate."

In the days that followed, Charles had ground penetrating radar brought to the site. The full extent of the find was revealed as the radar enabled us to look ten feet below the surface. This revealed an entire Roman Cavalry outpost, a complex of buildings that housed shops, barracks and command quarters for at least four hundred soldiers. According to Charles' research into Roman Cavalry strategies, these outposts were used as a base of operations until the army conquered the local area and forced the Celts to swear allegiance to the emperor. Then the unit would move on to conquer a different area, leaving the outpost as a temporary depot for supplies or troops moving through the empire.

CHAPTER 8
Instant Celebrity

I became an instant celebrity in England, and somewhat famous in the archeology community. My university asked me to stay in England longer to work on the mapping and the initial archeological preparation of the site. My PhD dissertation would focus on our finds but omit how I had found it. Ann returned to California but we kept in touch by letters, emails and long phone calls. Over the next few months, Charles and I worked closely together and he became my mentor and guide. Our professor-to-student relationship was enhanced with a genuine friendship.

In the following months, I remained in England and often visited with Charles at his home in Norwich. His wife, Claire, seemed excited to have a famous young American as a frequent houseguest. Ever smiling and lively, Claire's tasty cooking and loving personality made me feel like one of the family. Being away from home for all these months, this family togetherness became food for my homesick soul.

One night, months into the cavalry post dig and after devouring one of Claire's tasty homemade dinners, Charles and I went into his study. He meticulously started a fire in a brick fireplace. Waves of warmth flowed into the room in harmony with the crackling of the flames. The chills of the English winter, cold and damp, made me long for those hot summer days of our first exploration of the site. His study looked both like a library and a museum. Books, artifacts, pottery neatly placed on shelves, muskets and swords mounted on the walls, signified Charles scholarly pursuit of ancient history as well as his love of order and detail.

"Charles, we've talked about this before but I need to know what your opinion is about my vision that led to the find. It comes back to haunt me now and then. I have to say, my experience wasn't a vision. I actually had a full body experience. The water in the river felt real against my skin, I remember the shiver from its coolness, its texture, its taste, the way it bubbled into my nose and pressured against my sinuses. I had perspired from the hot day and I remember how cool the water felt when I dove under to wash off.

"That was me, I was there, it wasn't a dream or a vision, it was a rock solid reality," I said as Charles looked at me curiously. "My dear Elliot, I do believe you in what you just said," Charles leaned back in his red leather chair and smiled as he took out a pipe and pouch of tobacco. "So you do believe that I went back in time or something?" I put out my hand in a gesture of seeking his acknowledgement. He stopped smiling and leaned forward becoming very serious, "Listen, what happened to you was real, the proof of the site shows it. Call it a past life experience if you like, or a psychic phenomenon. Obviously, old boy, something profound happened to you. I believe you." "Thanks. Now tell me, am I going nuts? What really happened? I don't believe in reincarnation. Well maybe I didn't but after this, well, I just don't really know;" I leaned forward and asked sincerely, "Can this happen to me again?" "By Jove, I hope it does, and yes do take good notes. Imagine what you can add to the archeological record as a first hand observer of what we spend years digging through mud, rocks and dirt for," he leaned back again, filled and lit his pipe. "Need to tell you one more thing, Elliot." He puffed rapidly and smoke steamed around him like an old chimney.

"Damn, Charles, that tobacco is not good for you, you know that, don't you?" I asked both in jest and concern. "Not good for me physically, Elliot, but wonderful for me emotionally and spiritually, besides, it's pure tobacco, no additives," he said. "Whatever," I replied, "and…?"

"And, what?", he placed the pipe down for a second while I motioned for him to proceed with what he wanted to tell me. "Oh, yes, something similar happened to me, by no means as intense as your experience, but nonetheless, I did experience being another 'me' at another time," he said making eye contact.

"You did!" I leaned forward and touched his leg, "Well, go ahead, what, when, where, how, tell me, come on, don't hold back, let it rip," my excitement echoed through the study. "God, you Americans know how to get to the point, don't you," he puffed on his pipe again, more smoke rose around him.

"Well, two years ago, my bride of 30 years, Claire and I, visited an old Saxon church about a half mile from the shore on the North Sea. An ancient church, it was built we estimate around 900 AD, marvelous stone work, amazing that it's still standing, now a monument and not a working church," he stopped to puff again. He blew smoke up aiming toward the ceiling and watched it rise toward a window.

"Ahh, this tobacco is sublime, sure you don't want to try some?" Charles said. "No, no just keep going, I mean with your story, I can't handle suspense, Charles," I said pleading. "Really, Elliot, you must learn to contain your enthusiasm, not good for you, you know; all you Yanks, always in a rush," he said. I closed my eyes slowly and shook my head back and forth in response.

"Ok, well," he continued, "While Claire was off in the back of the church looking at some statuary, I walked up to the altar and stood there as if I were a priest. I closed my eyes and pretended I was a priest. For you know Elliot, I wondered what it would be like to be a man of the cloth? I stood there, perhaps for five minutes, imagining saying mass a thousand years ago. When I opened my eyes, the strangest thing happened. I looked out into the sanctuary. And, there, standing in front of me, stood noblemen and their ladies. Dressed in fine gowns, the women were lovely, their noble men in light armor and shining mail, standing right in front of me. They didn't have pews back then, you know, everyone stood for the service. This scene had to have happened over a thousand years ago considering the age of that church and the style of clothes everyone wore."

He moved his hand further out trying to give perspective to the scene he was describing, "behind them, stood the craftsmen and their ladies, iron workers, stone masons, hardy people. Then, in the back, way in the back of the church stood the peasants, farmers, in ripped old clothes with dirt on their hands and faces. What struck me most was neither the fancy dress of the nobles nor the intensity of the craftsmen, but the simple joy emanating from those farm peasants. Despite their apparent poverty, Elliot, they all had smiles on their faces. These poor lowly peasants were happy and fulfilled. As if, mother earth herself enfolded them in her arms, in gratitude for working the soil."

He paused for a moment as if taking in some momentous scene from a wonderful play in his memory. I remained quietly enthralled not only in his story but in that distant enchanting look on his face. "And on the altar, was a simple gold cup filled with wine and some bread. I looked down on them and felt a holy wonder in me a peace and contentment I've never experienced before or since. I wore simple vestments, the garb of a country priest." His enchanted gaze left him and he leaned back again in his red leather chair.

"Was that really you? I mean the priest, was it you?" I asked. "Oh, it was me alright, that I knew, I was there, but only for a few seconds. Amazing isn't it, what the mind can perceive, sense, almost intuitively, and process in just a few short seconds." Up came the pipe again; he puffed rapidly and smoke belched out like a steam engine.

"Claire called me while I stood there but I didn't hear her. Next thing I know, she's shaking my arm. Snapped me out of it she did." "How long did your vision last?" I asked. "Not a vision at all, like you said, it really happened, I could feel the vestments on me, I could smell the smells of the people. I had just consecrated the bread and wine. You know, Elliot, I could still taste the wine on my pallet," he paused long enough for me to ask, "During the experience or after?" I asked

"Strange thing, during the experience, I remember that clearly, the wine tasted good, locally grown grapes, strong intense flavor, not like the watered down stuff they call wine today. I'm a bit of a wine connoisseur, you know. So I know good wine when I taste it," he said waving his hand toward a wine rack in the corner, which I hadn't noticed before. "Charles, you constantly amaze me," I said.

"Of course, I'm quite knowledgeable for a poor scholar, you know, but I remember clearly that after Claire shook my arm and I came back to the present, the taste of the wine left my palette with the experience. Rather disappointing, for that wine tasted exquisitely fine," he put his head down as if he had finished a profound speech. "So you know what I mean when I spoke of my experience," I looked him straight in the eye. Although we had a growing friendship, a deeper sense of camaraderie came over us.

"Yes, I do and that's why I let you do 'your thing', as you Americans say rather quaintly. At our first dig campsite, your story of your vision fascinated me and so I uncharacteristically let you leave my well-structured team to jaunt around the English country side." He reached over to his desk and produced a business card, which he quickly handed to me. I read the card, Dr. Laura Duningham, Department Head, Quantum Physics, University of Norwich.

"You have an appointment with her tomorrow at noon at the university's science building. Be on time, she's quite busy, but she's looking forward to talking with you. I had to go through all sorts of gyrations to get an appointment with her on such short notice." Charles look went from his natural smile to a serious gaze.

"What the hell am I seeing a physicist for?" I burst out perplexed. "You'll find out and you may find the answer to 'what's going on'," Charles said as a smile came back to his face.

CHAPTER 9
Quantum Archeology

The next day, at 11:55 am, I sat down in a mahogany-walled conference room in the Physics Department at the University. "Dr. Duningham will be here shortly. Would you like some tea?" the administrative assistant of the department asked after she escorted me to the room. "Oh, no thanks, I'll just sit here and wait," I replied. 'England must float in tea,' I thought. I smiled and the secretary turned and walked back to the reception area. Old leather armchairs, dark wood walls, and heavy legged conference table that could seat eight people gave the room a comfortable academic look.

Right on time, Dr. Duningham walked into the room or should I say glided into the room. She moved with the speed and elegance of a figure skater. Her reddish auburn hair made her large blue eyes radiate. Her fitted dark red dress made her look like a member of the royal family and hinted at her feminine physique. Well groomed and dynamic, she commanded my immediate attention.

"Mr. Rizzo, how are you and welcome. Dr. Weldon spoke to me about your accomplishment and its origins. Quite a story," she said as we shook hands. Her firm grip added to her energetic presence. "Yes," I said as we sat down across from each other, "Nothing like this has ever happened to me before. Dr. Weldon told you the whole story about my vision which led to the Roman garrison discovery?" I asked.

"Yes, Dr. Weldon gave me all the details, but I'd like to hear it directly from you," she said. Her body erect, her hands folded together on the wood conference table; her attention focused totally on me. I felt honored at being the center of attention of this eminent professor. "Gladly," I said, "but before I start, one thing has me really confused," I said opening my hands in a sign of subtle surrender. "Yes, what's that?" she asked leaning forward slightly. "What am I doing here? This is the physics department and you are a premier quantum physicist and I'm an archeologist?" I raised and open my hands to emphasize the question. "Oh, I see, well that's easy to answer. But first tell me in detail your entire episode from start to finish then I'll explain why," she said.

I recounted to Dr. Duningham the dream vision in the park with Ann. I described being at the river and my view of the surrounding hills. I emphasized the body sensations I felt while swimming, indicating to her that my experience was not only in my mind but also in my body. She asked questions, forcing me to repeat certain scenes. She didn't take notes but listened intensely, her eyes focusing on me. This woman knew how to listen.

"Important question for you Mr. Rizzo," she asked, but feeling a bit uncomfortable with her formality and not used to being called 'Mr. Rizzo', I interrupted her. "Please, Dr. Duningham, call me Elliot." "Very well," she replied, "Elliot, when the voice called to you from the shore saying an important dispatch had just been received, what language did the person speak?" I sat there bewildered by her question; I'd never thought of that before, it just seemed logical that it was English. "Well, let's see, I understood him, so it had to be English. Right?"

"Think, Elliot. Your mind processes events in terms you can understand, but go back to that scene; what language did you ... hear? Try to remember the sounds, not the meaning." I sat back in my chair. Closed my eyes and drifted back to the scene: the double hill, the river, the cool refreshing water, and then, I just listened. I leaned forward, covered my face in my hands, and moved my index fingers into my ears not so much to shut out sound but to add emphasis to my mind to focus on hearing. Then there it was. I was back in the river and almost felt the water; I could see the double hills, feel my body cooling from the cold river water. I could hear the messenger calling to me and, then, I recognized the language he spoke. I popped up in my seat, energized by this discovery.

"Oh, my God, Doctor, it was Latin. Why didn't I notice that before?" I asked excitedly. Dr. Duningham asked, "What are the words you are hearing?" She reached around and grabbed a pad and pencil from a credenza and slid them over to me, motioning with her hand as if she was writing - her signal to me that this was important.

I lowered my head and played back the scene again. The words came slowly and I wrote them down as best I could. I looked up and said, "I could vaguely make out the words." I read from the yellow pad, "The voice said 'Centurus, praemitto efflagito concipio.' I'm vaguely familiar with Latin; I took two years back in high school." I shook my head, "but these words I heard are too complex and I have no idea what they mean."

"Try again," she asked. I closed my eyes and focused on that scene. The soldier's words were more distinguishable this time. Again, I wrote down exactly what I heard. She took the pad and pencil and read what I had written. An old fashioned phone sat on the credenza. She picked it up and dialed four numbers. "Grace, can you connect me with Dr. Fredericks in Language Arts, please. Thank you." Her voice inflected politeness and authority. A few seconds passed and she smiled, as I assumed, someone on the other side answered the phone. "Bill, how are you, Phyllis Duningham," she said and smiled as the other person answered and started some type of amusing conversation. Dr. Duningham smiled and nodded.

"Well, we'll beat their butts in football next game, don't you worry. And that should teach you not to bet so much money. But Bill, this is important; you're our Latin expert. What does: 'Centurus, praemitto efflagito concipio' mean?" After a few second pause, she wrote down something on her pad. "Thanks Bill, tea's on me next time, bye." She lifted her head toward me and smiled. "Quite amazing Elliot," she continued, "You truly had an alternate reality experience." She handed me the pad to show me what she had written. Under the Latin were the words: *Centurion, an urgent message has been received.*

"Wow!!" I said. I felt excited and victorious. However, some doubt lingered. "But why did I understand the message in English?" I asked. She leaned forward and spoke calmly, "Elliot, our minds understand concepts rather than words, plus you may have experienced bi-location, the mind sometimes acts as a bridge between dimensions." "Whoa, what do you mean by 'bi-location' and 'between dimensions?" I asked.

"Quantum Physics has shown us the same element of matter can and does exist in more than one place at the same time, that's bi-location. Also, that same element can exist simultaneously in two different moments in time, perhaps centuries apart, through what we call a Traversable Wormhole." I raised my hand in protest, "Whoa, again, what's a Traversable Wormhole?" "In due time Elliot," she leaned back and smiled, "I know this may sound confusing but try to follow me and it will all become clear. To get deeper, there are many dimensions higher than what our senses perceive as our 3 dimensional reality. These higher dimensions are beyond our understanding but we know through Quantum Physics that they do exist. OK?" she asked. "I'm all ears," I sat back into the comfort of the chair's open arms. I felt overwhelmed by all of this information and it felt more secure to collapse into the protective embrace of an old leather chair.

"I think now you'll also understand why Dr. Weldon sent you here. I'll explain this in layers, starting at the outer shell and if you're satisfied I need not go any deeper. But I can go deeper into the explanation if you want," she paused for my response. "I catch on easy, so start at the outer shell," I replied.

"An amazing aspect we have found during our experiments is the quantum field is somehow influenced by the presence of the observer, the one watching the experiment," she said still leaning forward. "And I became a Roman officer because…?" I leaned forward, too, opening up my hands slightly in a questioning motion. "This is only part of the theory; I've just explained how an observer, effects the reality, what he or she perceives as real. Mathematically, we can prove this but, and here comes the weird part, the math also shows that ours is not the only reality," she paused with that 'do you have any questions' look on her face. "I'm doing fine, please, don't stop," I pleaded.

"There are more realities, many more, in fact, billions. We call these realities possibilities. We can only perceive what goes on in our reality and only in our dimension within that reality; we can only guess about what goes on in the other dimensions, the other realities or possibilities, but we do know they exist," she continued. "Some possibilities may be variations of what we see as reality; some may be quite different. Let me add more," she said. "Now, it may well be those events from the past are in one of these possibilities or even what we call a parallel universe. We just don't know, yet." She smiled to emphasize the word – yet.

"We've had many stories, especially here in Europe by credible observers vividly seeing and experiencing historical events unfold right before their eyes. "For example, and this one should interest you," she paused. "A young family, wife, husband and young daughter, American tourists, were driving through Italy. They pulled over at a scenic overlook to view the enchanting valley below. Now, the road they were driving on was part of the old Apian Way, first built by the Romans over two thousand years ago. As they looked out over the valley below, the young girl turned around to the road and called to her parents; her voice alarmed them." Dr. Duningham paused. "Well, what did she see?" I asked somewhat annoyed that she stopped telling the story.

"There in front of them, an entire Roman Legion marched in perfect formation. Totally, awestruck, the father immediately thought a group of re-enactors had formed this troop. Then he thought that a movie, being filmed up the road, had sent these actors down the road for a scene being shot on film. But the column stretched on for nearly a half a mile, completely equipped with Roman banners, the Roman Eagle on a staff, officers on horses, chariots, wagons, and the whole legion following. The family said it was quite impressive.

"One of my colleagues was fortunate enough to hear about this event while also on vacation in Italy, for the family made quite a to-do about it and was interviewed in local news media. The husband, having served in the military himself, said the more he looked at these soldiers, as they were only a few meters away, he recognized they were real soldiers. The stern steady look, they marched in perfect cadence, weapons at the ready. But the wife, an observant woman, made the most startling observation," Dr. Duningham paused and surprisingly shifted subjects.

"Would you like some tea, err, Elliot," she asked with a concerned look in her eyes, "You look a little, woozy." "No, no tea; woozy, yes, this is fascinating, almost what happened to me, keep going, what did she observe?" I asked.

"Yes, the woman said that the knees of the soldiers, were below the surface of the road. It was as if, their road, the soldier's road was two feet or so below the present road. And that, Elliot, is the link between this event and what happened to you, when you heard someone talking in Latin," she paused. "The original Apian Way road bed, the road of two thousand years ago, of Roman times is two feet below the current road, which is raised due to ground swelling or some other reason. So the family observed a Roman Legion marching two thousand years ago, actually as it happened on the original road." "Did the soldiers see them?" I asked. "No, apparently the vision seems to be only one way," she answered.

CHAPTER 10
The Quantum Field

"That's a big difference from what happened to me. This family observed a past event. I lived it!" I said emphatically. "Allow me to continue," she replied, "first, in our dimension you can call what they saw a past event. But to the Roman soldiers, the event was quite present. You see, in the space-time continuum as described by Einstein, time is an aspect of our dimension. Leave our dimension and time, as we know it, doesn't exist. What we call the past is really happening right now, just in another reality. So, let's go deeper, shall we?" Her question being more like a directive.

"Yes, this is fascinating, almost as fascinating as archeology with which I thoroughly study the past; but now it seems Dr. Weldon and I are studying another reality," I said. "Not quite, in our reality it is the past but hop out of our reality, like you did back at the park and you are living our past," she said. Leaning forward again, "from what I can see, the family only made it to the periphery of the dimension boundary, if you will, while you, Elliot, actually went into the past, or other reality, and actually participated in it. Perhaps, the bi-location of Quantum Physics is at play here."

A whole new aspect of existence was opening up to me and I wanted to pursue this to its end or as far as Dr. Duningham could take me. "So why me," I asked. "Am I living in two realities? Or, if one believes in reincarnation, was I a Roman Centurion in a past life?" I asked. "It would appear that way," she answered.

After a pause, she leaned forward, "Now let's talk about the Traversable Wormhole." "Yes, let's," I responded, "I've been waiting to hear about this. What you've told me so far is starting to sink in. But I've heard about wormholes in Science Fiction movies and am interested on how it relates to my experience." Her demeanor became serious, "Important for you to recall Elliot, when you had your experience in the park, did you sense any sort of rotation or spinning at the beginning or end of your travel to the past?" I had explained my experience to Charles enough times that the answer rolled of my lips, "Why yes, I felt a counterclockwise spin as I traveled back in time and then a clockwise spin or rotation when I returned to the present. Does that mean anything?"

She smiled, nodded emphatically and nearly jumped out of her chair, "Yes! A Traversable Wormhole in action, good show, Elliot." Composing herself, she continued, "You see, one theory is that the Wormhole will spin one way as you enter it or travel in time and spin the other as you return. Your experience is extremely significant, Elliot. You are in a way confirming the Traversable Wormhole theory." Her words and enthusiasm settled me back in my chair; scientific theory was making my travel back in time as a Roman Centurion seem credulous.

"But why to that time?" I asked, "If there are some many parallel universes or possibilities. Why then?" Ever smiling, Dr. Duningham said, "Let me give you an analogy that may clarify this cross-reality experience for you. Say you're in a multi-cinema, you know, one of those movie houses that have ten theatres running movies at the same time, ten different screens, ten different audiences, ten different dramas going on at the same time. This is similar to the different realities in string theory," she paused for a second. "Good analogy, I understand, but how does my experience fit into this?" I asked. "Well, look at it this way. Say you leave your specific cinema and walk out into the lobby to go to the rest room. You walk back to your movie but get confused in the hall and enter the wrong cinema. You barge in, look at the screen and know you're in the wrong movie but it's a good show and you stay for a while. Finally, you know you have to leave because your friends or family in the original cinema will worry about you. So you leave and enter where you belong."

"Now this is what happened to you, when you fell asleep with your lady friend in the park that night. You left your cinema or reality and through the Wormhole, entered into another cinema or reality going on at the same time. The only difference between my analogy and your experience is that you were a performer and not in the audience. Nevertheless, you should see the similarity."

71

"Your analogy helps me understand the theory, but why did I leave my cinema, walk into another and then go back?" I asked. "I need you to re-evaluate what you mean by 'I'. The 'I' you talk about, your conscious self whom you call Elliot is the top of a very complex and deep subconscious iceberg that exists far below the surface of perceived reality," she said. "We are all new at this Elliot, we stand before a vast plain of infinite potential and multiple realities. We stand on a vast sea of Quantum Mechanics," she paused in near reverence. "Now that's a new term you just used but I think I've heard it before," I said. "What does it have to do with what happened to me."

"It has more to do with your mind, my mind, all of our minds. Quantum Mechanics tells us that a unified field of infinite potential exists below the subatomic structure. There are many theories about how it works. One approach compares our reality to an ocean. This ocean of being has waves of expression. Each wave is different but also part of the sea and we, my dear Elliot, are those waves. Our individuality rises and ebbs but is supported by this vast sea of infinite potential. Since we are one with it, we are one with each other, we all come from the same ocean of consciousness," she said.

"You said before that there is a bridge between the different dimensions. Is that bridge the unified field of Quantum Mechanics and Traversable Wormholes?" I asked. She smiled, "Charles said you are a bright one. That could very well be and somehow, during that night in the park, you fell asleep and crossed that bridge through the Wormhole.

Perhaps, being in the same location where you were two thousand years ago, the field where you were digging, the town, your lady friend, and so on, all had a part to play in placing your mind into the quantum sea, and somehow you were placed into a new reality, two thousand years ago." She looked at her watch. "Do we still have time," I asked? "Yes, yes, I do have a conference, but there is ample time for us," her look reassured me of her interest in my story and me.

"You know I didn't give much credence to reincarnation. Excuse me, I mean alternate realities, until this happened. Now I'm a firm believer. But why then? Why exactly at that time? Why did I land there and not a month later or sooner?" I asked again with hands raised in confusion. "I don't think it was a random event, or you wound up exactly at that place by happenstance. The quantum mind has infinite potential but also infinite intelligence. You were placed in that time and place for a reason by a deeper aspect of yourself. Perhaps, you will find out. Are you going back there, soon?" she asked. "No, I'm heading back to the States to finish up my doctoral thesis on finding the Roman fort, because of its location in Britannia, and its impact on the absorption of the Celtic tribes into the Empire," I answered. "You're somewhat of a celebrity here you know. The newspapers tell of the archeological find of the decade by an American. I must say you look better in real life than your photos do in the newspapers. And who, may I ask, is that young woman you were with?" her smile broadened.

"That's Ann, another American, and she's the one I was with when I had that inter-dimensional experience." I thought for a second. "Do you think she had something to do with it?"

"Could be, try again, and see what happens. I mean napping with her in the park. Keep in mind, the observer affects the outcome and that principle may come into play. Well I must go now, duty calls. Good fortune to you Elliot. It has been wonderful talking to you." We shook hands, I thanked her and she left.

I sat down and thought intently on what she had said. It all makes some sort of sense. Talking about it was not the same as the experience but talking put everything into perspective. My experience bordered on the unreal, the mysterious, the scary but, also, the fascinating. Dr. Duningham's explanation of Parallel Universes, Traversable Wormholes and Quantum Mechanics reassured me that I am part of a whole much larger infinite dynamic and, for now, offered an explanation of my experience. I could now put it to rest and continue with my career. It would, however, resurface again, much stronger and with gut wrenching fury.

CHAPTER 11
Two Years Later
At the Gilcrist Manor

Rebecca Gilcrist looked out from the bedroom window in her family manor where she now lived with her mother and brothers. The manor that had been in her family for countless generations overlooked the fields that lay a few miles south of the equally ancient town of Glastonbury. A jutting distant hill, its crown of rich trees brightened by the morning sun was visible through her bedroom window. The hill was long, running from left to right, and filled the width of the window. The surrounding low countryside magnified the protrusion of the hill. It could be seen clearly for miles around. Rebecca stared at it and knew its ancient secret that her family had kept for countless generations would soon be the focus of much attention.

For this reason, Rebecca had left her job as the Financial Director for a London based corporation and returned to her ancestral land. At twenty-eight, she had risen to an executive position with a significant salary and stock options. Her more envious co-workers say she got the position because of her long black hair, seductive green eyes and firm figure. But those who worked with her knew otherwise. Rebecca's bright and intuitive insights elevated the company's routine accounting practices to a new height. They could now calculate profit and loss trends accurately and quickly amidst the confusion of a failing economy. So revolutionary were her techniques that her company's profits rose ten percent instead of experiencing stagnating revenue as did its competitors.

As she put on her hiking boots for the climb up the hill, she remembered her company vice president's pleas for her to stay and not leave. "We'll increase your salary and bonuses Rebecca. Will that help? What are they offering you?" She looked at her boss with soft but steel-like eyes, "there is no 'they' Bill. I'm going back to the manor for personal family reasons and I can't have my head in one place and my heart in the other." Bill Robinson appreciated her honesty and graciously proposed, "OK, but we'll hold your position open for six months; call it a leave of absence. If you change your mind, call me, won't you?"

That memory faded for now as her concern that her family's ancient secret would soon be discovered. The archeologists would be here within hours and she had arrived late last night to help as best she could. She stared at the photo on the dresser. There stood her father in his RAF uniform his chest decorated with pilot's wings and rows of medals, the man she adored, killed when she was a teenager. Instantly, the memories of that day bolted through her like electricity.

The men in RAF uniform standing at the door; her hearing their words 'he crashed flying a search and rescue mission, all on board were killed;' her mother screaming, her brothers huddling in shock, she crying uncontrollably for days.

She snapped back to the present hearing her named called. "Rebecca, we're ready." Composing herself, she awakened from those memories to see her brother Steven, now the patriarch of the family, standing at the bottom of the stairway. He looked like a bear standing erect. His girth dominated the stairwell and blocked any view of the hallway below. Rebecca came bounding down the stairs, "Steven, you are just one big teddy bear. Can you still catch me after all of these years?" She giggled, reached the bottom of the stairs and jumped into his arms. "Sister, you're just one sweet little fairy queen. Thanks for coming from the big city to help us with this." Steven hugged her, "Come into the living room. Mother, Lance and Robin are waiting for us."

Anna Gilcrist sat as a queen in a large sofa like chair. Her poise and elegance balanced with a country woman's hardiness made her look ageless. At sixty-five, she looked more youthful than most woman of forty. Robin, the youngest Gilcrist, a junior in college and Lance, a former Royal Marine now local businessman, stood as they walked in. They greeted Rebecca with smiles and quick hugs, sat down, and asked about her trip and if she was enjoying her return back home. After a few pleasant exchanges, her mother moved the conversation to the purpose of their meeting. "I would like to discuss with you the coming changes to our way of life and changes that are emerging all over the world. We must ask the question—Is the world ready to know what is on our land?"

Everyone nodded but Lance said, "Mother, you've told us about our land and heritage since we were children. I admit we live in a wondrous place but I'm not clear on all its mysteries. Whenever asked, you seem to hold back, why?" Anna looked at Lance, "The time must be right for me to tell you certain things, for it is drawing close, very close." "Close, because of the archeologists?" Robin asked. "Let's lay it out logically. We know there are ruins at the top of the hill and you've all heard tales of St. Leo's stone, that wondrous large stone that helped him bring peace in ancient times after the Roman's left," Anna said.

Lance leaned forward in his chair, "Are you inferring, Mother, that the mythical stone is on our land also? It's supposed to be in a cave or something like that but I've hiked our land since I was a child and never ever found any caves." Anna said, "true, but terrain can change over the millennia. So perhaps it may be on our land or not." Anna was holding back the truth until her family's curiosity had grown. "So I propose we allow the archeologists access to the ruins on top of the hill as the satellite imagery has found the ruins directly and our site is now well known throughout the archeological community. I think there's enough on the hill to keep them busy for quite some time, then let events work out as they will, for we are in God's hands."

"I agree Mother but I feel you're holding something back from us. We have known of the ruins on top of the hill since we were children and we were sworn an oath not to tell anyone and we haven't. Yet…" before Lance could finish Robin jumped in, "yes but what of the mysteries we have heard about since our childhood." Anna replied, "in due time my children, within a week or so, all will be revealed to you. I ask your patience and trust." Lance said, "Mother, we're not children and…" Steven coughed out loud, "Listen, my siblings, mother knows the best way to handle this. So let us follow her directions."

Rebecca, overwhelmed with being back home and plunging into this family conclave summoned up the courage to say, "It is good, Mother, that you did not fight this in court. It would have only drawn more attention indicating we may have had something to hide." Anna replied, "yes with all of the interest in England's archeological past and everyone knowing that St. Leo did live somewhere around here, a storm of curiosity and questions would have risen as sure as clouds rise to fill the hot afternoon sky.

"And let's get to know our archeologist friends and keep close watch on their intentions. We'll invite them to the manor as we become more familiar with them. I feel strongly these are honorable and sincere men working for the best of intentions." Steven spoke up, "I have information about the two men leading the archeology team." Everyone turned to listen. Steven explained that he had met Dr. Charles Weldon at The Legend Pub in the village last night. "We enjoyed a thoughtful chat about ancient ruins and the history of the countryside. Of course I only spoke in generalities. Good chap this Charles, I liked him the minute I saw him, its like I've known him before. He has only the purest interest in our history and for finding out the truth to be shared with all."

"And what about the other?" Anna asked. "A Yank, damn good archeologist, extremely fluent in Roman Britannia, knows more about the UK's history than most of us. Dr. Weldon brought him over here because of his extensive knowledge of the Roman and early Christian era of Britain. He's the one who made that find of the Roman Cavalry fort east of here. Remember all the attention it got in the news?" Steven said.

"Yes, is that him? The news called him the Roman Yank, Hah! Now he's going to be here on our land. If there are mysteries or caves on our land, he'll find them for sure," Lance said as he shook his head. Steven looked directly at Rebecca, "Oh, and one more thing, he's young, single, successful and quite a catch."

"What are you looking at me for? I'm not interested in any man, especially an American, my big brother," Rebecca jokingly sneered at Steven and poked him in the arm. "Oh, my little sister, I'm just looking out for you, besides I would like some little nieces and nephews running around here," Steven laughed.

"Yes sister, what are you waiting for?" Robin joined in. "Think of us, we need some children to spoil," Lance added. "Mother!" Rebecca sought Anna's intervention. "It does me good to see you all together and laughing. It tells me I did a good job and that our family's ancient secret still blesses us." Lance leaned forward, "There you go again Mother, what secrets?"

To meet his challenge, Anna leaned forward and for a few seconds stared into Lance's eyes, "mark my words Lance, the Royal Marines have not even come close in preparing you for what you will be experiencing within the next week. Your life will change dramatically." Lance, somewhat deflated, sat back and sighed. Without losing her momentum, Anna turned, "Rebecca, take Robin with you to meet the archeologists. Be courteous but also somewhat naive; act as if you don't know anything about the hill or the ruins. Is that clear?" "Yes, Mother." Rebecca and Robin answered in unison.

CHAPTER 12
The Adventure Begins

"Good morning, here is your contract and car keys Dr. Rizzo. Enjoy your stay in England," the rental car agent said as she handed them to me. "Thanks, I always do, beautiful country you have here." I slung my backpack over my shoulder and walked to the rental car lot. I went through the mental drill of preparing myself to drive a vehicle with the steering wheel on the right side while I drive on the left side of the road. I had to adjust quickly, the clock in the car glowed 7 AM. In order to meet with Professor Charles Weldon, my friend and colleague, at 11 AM, I had to drive quickly to meet him at the hotel he had booked near our new site.

Also running through my mind was Charles' phone call last week. "We think we have an unusual find, Elliot. One of the university's research teams while going over satellite imagery, found a potential site in western England near Glastonbury. Can you come over here and assist in my first visit to the site. Your intuitive insights will go a long way in determining if it is worth the University's time and resources to excavate."

And why did he call me? Well in the two years since our first meeting, the site I discovered then yielded secrets and new information about the Roman occupation of ancient England. Further research based on the site artifacts revealed much about the life in the Roman cavalry. I had completed my doctorate and published my first book about the find that became an overnight success and catapulted me into media fame as an explorer, archeologist and adventurer, a modern Indiana Jones. Of course, I never mentioned my other-reality vision experience.

While I appreciated the acclaim the cavalry fort find bestowed on me, the truth is I'm just an archeologist who happened to tap into a dimensional rift during a dream vision. Being fair, that's probably worthy in itself of media attention, although I had no conscious control over how it happened. To go on, I am a natural in discovering more data about Roman occupied Britannia. My interests had shifted to early Christian Britannia and the overlap in the history between the slow growth of Christianity and the departure of Roman influence.

As I drove away from London, I remember Charles' note to me: This site may be a bit tricky to get to see as it's on a private estate. The family has been there as long as recorded history so I will need all the support I can get to persuade them to let us explore and potentially excavate the site. The drive, thru traffic and west toward Glastonbury, involved dodging some rush hour traffic before settling into the pleasant rural lanes of the countryside. Charles, waiting for me in front of the hotel, climbed into the car, suspended many of his social pleasantries as he motioned for me to follow the road that would take us to our potential site.

"We just have enough time to drive there and meet them. The site is about seven miles south," Charles said as he hopped into my car. "Who is 'them'?" I inquired as I turned onto a road he had motioned me toward. "The Gilcrists, they own the land, as I wrote in my brief note to you. They will be at the site to escort us around. I've surmised in my initial dealings with them that they are very private people. I met Steven Gilcrist last night in the local pub, an amiable chap; he gave me a brief background of his family, his mother Anna, and the heritage of their manor and their land. He suggested we meet at the site this morning. So all seems well."

"By the way, and changing the subject, not bad for a Yank." Charles said. "Are you referring to my driving?" I said as I consciously strained to keep my rental car on the 'British side of the road'. "That and your latest paper on Roman outposts in Scotland and how the Romans may have paved the way for the growth of Christianity. Very good conclusions and based on evidence that others in the field have found but have not used to reach your conclusions. Where do you get your insight?" Charles asked. He gripped the strap over the door as we turned off the main road onto the dirt drive that would take us near the site. The rental car took the bumps and furrows well. The narrow road, surrounded by miles of meadow and farmland, wound up the hill like a river, and appeared to end a mile ahead where a grove of trees crowned the top of the hill.

"I read the news of recent archeological discoveries, do a little research on my own, cross reference other reports and then it just comes," I said. "Just comes?" Charles demanded. "Not as intense as my dream two years ago, nothing as intense as that. Call it intuition, creative writing or whatever, but it just happens, Charles. I get notions, feelings, write it down and then it comes: a story on Roman garrison life that everyone marvels at. I know the dream helped in some way," I said. "You remember that story you told me about being in that old church? You felt like you'd been there hundreds of years ago. That's happening to me more and more. Plus, I'm interested in early Christianity in Britannia and have been researching the early missionaries. What do you know about St. Leo?"

"Ah, St. Leo also referred to as Brother Leonidas, I knew you would find him fascinating. Quite the subject to talk about, he was considered a mystic, did much healing work but now is not the time to talk about him. Let's stay focused on what's ahead of us," Charles responded. "Ok but maybe he is or was what's ahead of us, maybe these ruins are his church supposedly located around here and…" but before I could say more Charles interrupted me to describe his meeting with Steven Gilcrist and as the oldest brother, what he had learned about the family and their request for privacy.

"And by the way, his younger sister, Rebecca, is your age and quite a looker from what I've been told. Are you and Ann, is it, still an item?" I turned to Charles. "You mean Ann from my first dig? We broke up a few months ago," I answered and could feel a wave of relief and sorrow come over me. Strange this falling out of love and the complex emotions that remain. "We didn't seem to have any spark anymore. Being on two different coasts in the US didn't help either. Our phone conversations grew shorter. The silence in between sentences grew longer; I had to grope for something to say. We both sensed the growing separation and decided to call it off. Haven't heard from her since, she wanted it that way, a complete break."

"And no, after Ann, I'm not interested in looking at another woman," I said. We hit a bump and then a hole in the road, the car bounced, interrupting our conversation. Charles continued, he laughed and slapped his knees. "Really, hah, what do you yanks say, 'never say never'?" Just then, we came to a point where the road dipped and turned then climbed a slight hill. I had to turn the steering wheel hard to the left.

"Wow, this is going to be a tough one," I said as I slowed. "Hold on." I down shifted as we took the curve, dip and climbed up the hill, with a bounce the car almost tipped, all four wheels digging into the dirt road and spraying out dirt and rocks. We skidded for a moment but then the road was smooth again. "Good driving, ole man," Charles said. We bounced along as the road turned into a trail with just a few inch clearances on either side of us. I slowed down again apprehensive of the narrowing road and where it would end.

"Keep going, Elliot. According to Steven Gilcrist, this trail should end in a small clearing hundreds of feet from the summit. They will be waiting for us and we'll need to walk the rest of the way from there." The trail ended by a stand of trees where a red pickup truck came into view a few yards ahead at the roads end. We stopped, and while unbuckling seat belts and unpacking our camera and gear, I noticed a young man and an attractive woman standing by the truck. "She's stunning, Charles. What a knockout," I said. I didn't want to stare at her. They both waited with the demeanor of British royalty.

"She's the Gilcrist daughter. Rebecca is her name and she's recently arrived from London. Control your testosterone my young American cowboy we need to make a very cordial and polite first impression and remember, what you told me, you're not interested in a new romance," Charles replied. "Did I say that?" I paused. "And that's her brother, I presume?" "Yes, besides Steven, she has 2 brothers, Robin and Lance, I believe. Don't know which one that young chap is," said Charles.

I stepped out of the car and looked away from her. I could feel myself falling into her spell. Maintaining my focus on the summit of the hill a hundred feet ahead of us scanning for any type of structure brought me back to my senses and a professional demeanor. The hill appeared more to be the top of a ridge, which seemed to extend north to south for quite a distance. The trees or should I say 'the forest' covering all of the hilltop were surrounded by low-lying honeysuckle bushes, their smell creating an enchanting aroma. The trees and bushes concealed any structure from visibility. The whole area was simply delightful. To add to all of this charm, a warm sun shone as it continued its daily commute to the west; a steady breeze blew from the east; fresh and clear, carrying that hint of honeysuckle.

I pivoted around and gazed down at the quiet countryside below the hill. I imagined that at the summit one would behold a 360-degree panoramic view for miles in every direction. I turned to Charles, "If I was a Roman commander, this is where I would build my fort." Charles also gazing at the serenity of the hilltop and of the surrounding countryside said. "And if I were a Christian missionary, this is where I'd build my church." We looked at each other, nodded in agreement and laughed briefly.

As we turned and walked toward our hosts, Charles put his hand on my shoulder, "Elliot, my boy, something tells me this will be the dig of a lifetime." Charles' statement would prove to be true beyond our wildest dreams. We walked up to the Gilcrists and Charles performed the introduction formalities. I shook Robin's hand, his shake firm and strong, reflecting the masculinity that radiated from his powerful frame. Rebecca offered me her hand. She was absolutely gorgeous. Our eyes locked for a second more than appropriate for a meeting between a British woman with an ancient ancestry and an American with a cowboy flair for archeology. Like a computer downloading reams of information in one second, our eye contact seemed to transfer unspoken thoughts and feelings. I felt like I had known her all my life.

I normally get a little nervous when I first meet a beautiful woman until my internal pep talk mechanism kicks in. With Rebecca, a myriad of thoughts flowed through me. I felt a strong attraction and desire toward her but also a sense of unease, the source of which I could not identify. I decided to let go of all these feelings and allow them to work their way out. We turned and walked toward the trees. "Nice of you to show us around," Charles said. "Yes, our pleasure. We've never been to the top of this hill, so I don't know what to expect," Robin replied. As we walked up the hill, somehow to my apparent enjoyment, Rebecca wound up trudging along beside me.

CHAPTER 13
Ruins on the Hill

"I was told you're an American, have you explored many sites in England? I thought you'd prefer to be out in the Wild West digging up ancient burial grounds?" she asked. I was fascinated by her charm, and the interest she showed in me. I'm the kind of guy who likes the spotlight and will grab it whenever I can get a chance. Although, not an egotist, I like telling my own story. When someone shows a sincere interest in my work, especially a woman, well it is like having my own cheerleading section.

Before I could answer, Charles stepped in, "Elliot is one of the premier archeologists on Roman and early Christian times. He won't tell you that as he's quite shy and modest." "Actually Charles is the premier archeologist, I just happened to be around when he makes his finds," I said trying to cut him off at the pass.

"Don't let him fool you, Rebecca, excuse me, May I call you Rebecca?" Charles asked. "Why yes, that's fine, thank you for asking," Rebecca said with a slight smile obviously enjoying the academic banter. "Yes," Charles continued, "Don't let my distinguished colleague from America trick you into thinking he's new at this. For behind his young face is really a wise old man." We all walked slowly toward the site on a grassy meadow. "And," I added, "don't let Charles' looks deceive you either, Robin and Rebecca, for behind that wise old man's face is a much much older, really old man. In fact, Charles, often digs up his own past at many of the sites he works at." "Sounds like you two have worked together before," Robin said. "Yes, I work, Elliot just shows up," Charles said. "OK you two that's enough," Rebecca said. She had seen and been a part of enough co-workers joking to enjoy the teasing. We continued to walk toward the trees, with Robin and Rebecca now taking the lead while Charles and I fell noticeably behind.

"She's absolutely gorgeous. Charles, I think I'm falling in love," I whispered. "Down boy, think of your career, think of all those beautiful seductive woman you've yet to meet," Charles said. "Besides, I always meant to tell you that true archeologists do take a four word oath, Sex – No…." I looked at him with exasperation and just said, "Sex, No." "That's exactly the point my dear young American friend," Charles said, "Sex no, dig yes." "This is it." Robin said, "Not much here." He turned around and a look of surprise came over him when he saw how far behind we had lagged.

Once I'm near a dig site some unseen force like the instinct of salmon to swim upstream takes over. I walked past the first trees, which stood like sentries guarding an unseen kingdom. Robin, Rebecca and Charles followed me but

I walked faster pulled by this invisible force. "Stand back folks, the hound is on the trail," Charles said. I navigated around shrubs and tree branches taking in the terrain for hidden signs of walls, toppled towers, or abutments.

Unseen from the road and well hidden behind the line of trees laid an area with low shrubs dotted with towering ancient trees. The area, which I assumed to be part of a much larger complex, seemed to be about half the size of a football field and it lay hidden from view, totally invisible from where we had parked. Surrounded on all sides by high trees, the clearing nestled by itself resembled a sanctuary, totally obscured from view from anywhere in the surrounding countryside. A wave of peace came over me as I walked into this clearing, a similar feeling I get when I walk into ancient sites in England. But this felt different and that 'I've been here before feeling' started to creep into me.

About 40 meters away, I could see the outline of two buildings, their walls protruding up from the ground and partially hidden by undergrowth. I walked faster, and then faster still. A rush of energy flowed through me as I ran toward the ruins, maneuvered around three foot high shrubs and low hanging branches as no clear path to the ruins existed. "This is it Charles," I yelled back at him as he, twenty meters behind me, trotted along tryin to keep up. Robin and Rebecca trotted behind him so as the three of them formed a line jostling in and out of the shrubs. The walls protruded six feet out of the ground in some places and only two feet in other areas. In some places, there was no wall at all. But I could clearly see the outline of a building that could easily have been an early Christian church. I quickly calculated its size, ten meters wide by twenty-five meters long.

"Looks like an open structure," Charles said as he finally caught up with me. "Early Christian, could be, heh?" "Let's look at the masonry," I said.

We walked up to the highest wall segment and were barely aware of Robin and Rebecca who, for some reason, now only seemed mildly interested and stood well back from us. "Early mortar holding field stones together, typical period construction," I said. We both stood a few feet back from the wall slowly walking the perimeter of the building looking for how the stones were bonded together, for icons that may have been built into the wall, as well as other telltale signs indicating its age and origin.

I heard Charles bellow out a "Damn it!" and turned just in time to see him trip and fall sideways flat onto the ground. He sat up quickly and before I could laugh and make a cross cultural joke, he looked up and with that 'O shit, no more fooling around look' that came over him, he pointed a shaking finger at me, "Don't you dare." he said."Ok, ok, truce," I said restraining myself and then turned my head away and laughed out loud making sure he heard me. "Elliot, you promised not to…" he stopped talking as he looked at what he had tripped over.

"Look here, what do you make of this?" Charles now kneeling, pointed with his left hand to what appeared to be a round carved stone sticking out of the ground at an angle. Then he placed his right hand on a much longer stone pointing out of the ground about two feet from the first. Both stones appeared to have been worked; their smooth surfaces showed shallow carved lines and they protruded up from the ground at a ninety-degree angle from each other.

Charles moved his right hand downward from the second carved stone and his left hand from the stone he tripped on toward his right hand. The imaginary lines he inscribed intersected exactly at a ninety-degree angle. I raised my right fist and yanked it down in the popular gesture of triumph. "Yes, yes!" I screamed, "great work Charles. I take back all of those remarks I just said about you."

"Hold on old man, still not confirmed, but I think you're right," Charles said as he stood up and shook my hand. Without speaking a word aloud, we both knew we had found the large stone symbol of Christianity, a large cross carved from stone.

Robin and Rebecca still standing where they first entered the ruins, left their place and abandoned their seemingly indifferent posture to run up to us. Their previous disinterest now replaced with an intense curiosity. "Looks like we found a cross, its buried with only the two tips protruding out of the ground, we need to dig it out to confirm its style and eventual age," I said. "Yes, still preliminary and we have weeks maybe months of work but it looks like we may have an early Christian church here," Charles said.

"The church of Saint Leo?" Rebecca asked. "Don't know yet, we really need to dig deep for that, 400 AD was a long time ago," Charles said. "Yes, of course," she said, "Well I have to speak to our mother about this, as she must decide if this land is to be dug up or remain untouched and sacred as it is." Ever the diplomat, Charles said, "I understand. There are various ways we can approach our research here so as not to disturb too much. But you do see the possible incredible importance of where we're standing right now." "Yes, we do," Rebecca said, "but understand our position, we are concerned about tourists, news media, with cameras, additional traffic. We are very private people Dr. Weldon and we'd like to keep it that way as much as we can."

Robin walked up to Rebecca and stood next to her. The two stood together projecting a silent strength of unity. I sensed immediately a deep family bond. I also, saw Rebecca in a different light. Standing in the ruins she glowed like a goddess. She stood erect, strong yet elegant, slim but graceful. She radiated, beauty, innocence, strength and resolve. I felt awe, desire and intimidation and wanted more of a relationship with her but felt inadequate, like a teenager with a crush on a movie star.

I knew without a doubt that I had to change this feeling and change it immediately. The phrase 'A weak heart never won a fair maiden' echoed in my mind. I wanted her in any way I could have her and I knew she was wanted by a hundred other men. She could easily sense a babbling faint-hearted approach to get to know her. I need to find my warrior self soon or a bashful schoolboy demeanor would over take me. At this point,

I decided to be authentic and professional, do my job, calculating the risks as well as the opportunities; she owned the land I'm about to dig on and there's plenty here for me to absorb.

I often marvel on how fast the human mind can process such information. She was still talking to Charles and her personality shifted to a land baroness in less than two sentences of their conversation. Then it happened. Something caught my eye in the wall behind them and broke my trance sending a chill right through me. Our research into this structure was just about to advance and I may now get to know Rebecca better.

"Yes, I understand, but we will control who and when people could come to the site. We've done this so many times before that…" Charles never finished his consoling sentence to Rebecca. "Oh my God, Charles, look," I shouted as I ran to the wall adjacent to where we were standing. Barely containing my enthusiasm, I touched the wall like an art student touching the Mona Lisa. "Yes, yes, Charles, look at all of this. Damn, nearly the whole base of the wall." Charles rushed to stand next to me. "God, Elliot do you know what this means?" I knelt and followed the wall's telltale structure into the ground.

"What is going on, what did you find?" Robin stood next to Charles while Rebecca knelt next to me. "Tell me Elliot, it looks just like a wall to me. What did you find?" She said truly interested in what had excited me. "Flat brick," I said. "What?" Robin said "…Long and flat…" Charles mumbled. "Long flat brick," Rebecca said, "and…?" I replied, "Don't you see what this means. The only people who used this type of masonry were the Romans." I looked at her to help her draw out the answer to what we had found. "So, what do you think that means Rebecca?"

"That the Romans had something to do with building this wall," she said. "Yes, exactly, very good," I said to encourage her on. "Now take the next jump in logic and what do you get?" "That this is more than an old Christian site," she said running her hand across the wall. She turned to me with an inquisitive look, her deep green eyes searching for confirmation for what she was about to conclude, "It is Roman, too!"

Robin looked at his watch. "Well, I think we're at our limit here gentlemen, time for us to leave, although I think we accomplished much here." Charles seemed somewhat withdrawn but slowly responded, "Yes, yes quite so. What do you say Dr. Rizzo?" I hesitated a bit, I really didn't want to leave, I could have stayed here for the rest of the day, "Sure, Charles, but why the rush to leave here?"

Rebecca politely added, "In a way, I agree Elliot. But, I think our mother must get involved now. Seeing how the legacy of this site appears to be so profound. Can we meet tomorrow at our home, the Gilcrist Manor?"

CHAPTER 14
Driving Back from the Ruins

We left Rebecca and Robin at the top of the hill and set a time to meet at the Gilcrist Manor at 10:00 am the next morning. As we walked to our rental car, Charles said, "Let me give it a try old chap, I need to drive." We drove from the site, waving farewell to the Gilcrists who politely waved back. Charles skillfully navigated down the dirt access road that connected the hill to the main motorway. "Charles, we just stumbled across a double find. An early Christian church on top of Roman ruins. Thanks for inviting me to be a part of this survey. We have a wonderful opportunity here, and maybe, just maybe the Christian ruins are remnants of St. Leo's mission from the 5th century," I said.

The words of my history professor back in graduate school popped into my head, 'Next to St. Patrick, St. Leo had the greatest impact on western Britannia. He brought not only Christianity to the Celts, but he filled the gap the Roman's left. He encouraged cooperation, peace reigned here for many years after he founded his church, until the Northern Europeans migrated into Britain.'

"So what do you think about the site?" I asked. Charles didn't answer me; he maintained his focus on the road like a racecar driver at the Indy 500. "Charles, did you hear what I just said?" I asked. But he didn't answer. "Hellooo," I said, "anybody home?" as I poked his left arm. "Sorry, Elliot, deep in thought, what did you just say?" he mumbled. He always jumped into any conversation about history or archeology. His lack of enthusiasm concerned me.

"What is it Charles, what's bugging you?" "You know, something damn peculiar happened to me back there," he said. "Yeah, I know she's attractive, intelligent and, I presume, available but Charles you're a married man," I said poking his arm again. Taking his eyes off the road for a quick glance, he turned toward me, "there you go, again, a slave to your hormones. Mine left me a few years back although I do agree with you about Rebecca." "So what peculiar thing happened?" I asked.

"Do you remember the story I told you, a few years ago about my experience at the altar in the old stone Saxon church by the North Sea?" he asked. "How could I forget, that helped me keep my sanity after I had my own parallel reality experience," I surprised myself, the words 'parallel reality experience' didn't feel odd or strange anymore. I had actually assimilated the belief of parallel lives, bi-location and wormholes into my worldview. The way the words were spoken, so matter-of-fact and so accepting of their truth, made me realize how I now believe that there may be other 'me's' somewhere living their own lives in other times. "Elliot, it started to happen again," he said. "What triggered it?" I asked.

By now we were on the main motorway heading back to our hotel. "Remember when you were pointing out the concrete at the bottom of the wall showing the delineation of the original Roman structure. It happened then, for a few seconds, I stood not under the trees with all of us but in the actual chapel. I could see the whole bloody place, the walls, doorways and the stone floor. Yes, the stone floor, I could feel the cold in my feet, I had on only sandals. I looked down at my feet, I could see the sandals and, and I wore a robe and held a staff. Oh, Elliot, I'm getting dizzy, I'm pulling over to the side of the motorway." He placed his directional signals on and came to an abrupt stop on the shoulder barely safe from traffic.

I pulled out a bottle of water from our gear, "Here, have a drink, relax, slide over here, I'll drive back," I said. Truly concerned about my friend and mentor and knowing what he must be feeling, I twisted off the bottle cap and gave the bottle to Charles. I opened the car door and walked around to the driver's side while he slid, somewhat clumsily, into the passenger's seat. After I buckled my seat belt and adjusted the mirrors, I checked for traffic and pulled out onto the motorway, swerving a bit as I accelerated. "Oh, God, my life is in the hands of an American driving a car in England. Angels protect me," he said faking a bit of terror in his voice. "Quiet, before I really scare you," I responded as I sat back and slid the seat to a more comfortable position. "How do you feel?" "Still woozy, a bit, quite an experience, its hitting me more now. I feel disoriented as if I don't recall who I am now. I'm more attached to whom I was standing in that old chapel," he said. "Oh, ah, turn right up there at that round-a-bout, that road will take us straight to the hotel."

"That's what happened to me, I know that feeling of disorientation, like being caught between two worlds," I said, then added, "literally traveled between two realities. Did you feel any sort of spinning sensation like I did? Dr. Duningham called that rotation entering a 'Traversable Wormhole.'" "No, strange, I didn't feel that at all. I guess that rotation doesn't always happen," he replied. "Dr. Duningham has done more research since you spoke to her last," Charles' voice became more relaxed. "What did she learn?" I asked. "Well something I can just confirm. People who have had multiple experiences with parallel realities report their most recent experiences seem more real than their first or second. They become more deeply immersed in the other self, or past life, and that their transition back to their current life or reality takes longer, along with periods of disorientation," Charles said.

"And that's what's happening to you? But hasn't ten years past from your first experience, the one in the old church?" I asked. "Yes, but such a profound experience it was, I remember it clearly and now this one. Lord, I've been a priest twice in past lives," he said. "Aha! So that explains it all," I said. "Not now Elliot, this is serious," Charles shot back. "Ok, I know, couldn't resist it," I said skillfully pulling into a parking space in front of the hotel. "Do you think you're back here to find out who you were?" I asked. "I don't know. I don't know what's going on. All I know is that these experiences bewilder me. But I tell you, Elliot, they are a gateway into the past. If it happens again to me, or to you, let's take copious notes. They are a window into the past; we can learn much. So let's take advantage of them. Ok?"

He paused and took a deep breath, unbuckled his seat belt and opened the car door, "I'm starting to feel better now."

CHAPTER 15
Checking into the Hotel

At the front desk, the innkeeper smiled and gave me my room key. "Enjoy your stay here Dr. Rizzo. The professor here has taken care of all the paperwork. Breakfast tomorrow starts at 6:30 am. And, for your pleasure, early dinner is now being served." I smiled back and thanked the innkeeper.

We sat down to a traditional English dinner. I unceremoniously gobbled down my food. The traveling, the hill, meeting Rebecca, Charles' experience as well as the driving gave me the appetite of a starving lion. Charles ate quietly and I sensed his mind still floated in a fog from his priest experience on the hill.

After we ate, Charles took my arm and motioned me toward a sitting room, "Let's talk about tomorrow." The room, quite spacious, held enough ambiance to help bring Charles back to our time. The bookshelves, woven carpet and leather chairs resembled his study and that helped him regain his composure. "In our meeting tomorrow, I think we should be quite open and candid with the Gilcrists," Charles said.

I let him talk and direct the discussion. He needed to do this. Within minutes Charles became his old self again. "We should tell them we need a more thorough preliminary survey of the site. I want to get the scope of what we have here, wall heights, types of construction, out buildings, roads and paths, whatever we can find. Do you agree?" he asked.

"Definitely, good idea. But something else concerns me, Charles," I said. "What's that?" he asked. "The Gilcrists? I just find it hard to believe that they didn't know about these ruins before now? Think about it, farmers live off of the land and need to make use of every square foot of it. The site we looked at today had take up many acres. Albeit, on a long slopping hill, don't you find it curious that they didn't know about the ruins?" I asked. "Yes, but what about the site you found at Horningsham east of here, that was huge and the land owners didn't know about it?" he said. "Not the same thing," I responded. "First, the landscape had completely covered that site. We now know that area floods often. The river must have overflowed numerous times in the last two millennia covering all those buildings in silt. Plus that family didn't go back before recorded history like the Gilcrist's."

Charles shifted in his chair, the leather making a short belching sound. I couldn't turn down this chance, "Did you just pass gas?" I asked. "Old leather, my young man, old leather, does it all the time. Now, if you're finished with your juvenile humor, I'll proceed. About the Gilcrists, they're old traditional landowners and want their privacy, no one meddling around, right? Then we come along, with satellite imagery, pinpointing the site to within a square meter. How could they object without looking odd, stopping the discovery of valuable English artifacts and closing the door on an important part of history?" Charles paused for a second, contemplating his next words. "I agree with your concern but let's see how it unfolds. Right now they're cooperative but let's proceed politely and cautiously."

We concluded with the plan to follow at tomorrow's meeting at the Gilcrist's manor house; Charles left for his room while I went for a walk. Again, Rebecca kept popping into my mind. Why did I instantly become attracted to her? In fact, I realized that I could feel her presence, if you will, when Charles and I drove up to the hill. Had I known her from somewhere else or, possibly, from some other time? The walk invigorated me. The town with its centuries-old houses, quaint shops, mystical history, the legendary Glastonbury Tor and captivating cathedral ruins gave me a warm and secure feeling. As I walked down Magdalene Street I stopped for a moment to take in the mystery of the Glastonbury Abbey ruins. Walking by Abbey Park, a déjà-vu feeling came over me and I thought about my lucid dream in the park with Ann years ago.

I returned to my room, I showered and decided to spend the rest of the evening reviewing the topographical maps of the county that Charles had given me, as well as the satellite photos of the hill. I lay in bed and switched on my bedside reading lamp. I studied the Somerset county terrain maps and saw that our site sat on a hill, which was part of a two-mile long ridgeline. The site occupied the highest point on the north section of the ridge hence the name 'hill'. The ridge south of the hill sloped down gradually. If the Romans felled the trees closest to the site, they would have a panoramic view twenty miles in all directions. I studied the satellite photo and could see the road we drove up on the south slope of the hill and the flat area where we parked. The faint outline of ruins peeked out from the trees on the flat top of the hill. 'Amazing how they caught this,' I thought 'you can barely make out only part of one building.'

I began to feel drowsy, barely able to keep my eyes open. I stuffed the maps and satellite photo together into a folder, rolled over and switched off the night lamp. Visions of Rebecca's smiling face and elegant manners came to me as I fluffed my pillow to a soft marshmallow texture and I collapsed back onto the welcoming mattress. I wondered what it would be like to hug Rebecca the way I hugged my pillow. I dosed off smiling.

Within seconds, it happened, that falling vortex experience, the downward clockwise spiraling I experienced during my first dig. Then came the noise like a waterfall. Faster I spun into a deeper level of consciousness, asleep, but still awake and aware. Aware of noises getting louder and louder, distant shouts of men calling out in muffled voices. I knew I was going back in time, back again to the place of my previous dream; I spun into a deep dark well. And then I saw it, a point of light and it grew larger, and larger, it resembled a porthole. Was it the other end of the wormhole? Distant sounds became louder and louder. I tried to focus and become more alert. If this is another past life, I want to observe what's going on and remember every detail. Charles said this could be a blessing, a portal into the past, I could learn so much, if I could only hold on to self-control and whatever I could remember.

CHAPTER 16
My Second Time Travel

I fell deeper, more lights appeared, but the lights didn't spin, they were steady. The distant sounds became louder and, now I could hear voices. I became scared, disoriented. I'm plummeting into some time, some place and I have no control over what's happening to me. But I held on. I focused and gradually became more alert. I wanted to observe what was happening and remember every detail. I repeated to myself: Charles said this could be a blessing, a portal into the past. I could learn so much. Then, like being sucked into a vacuum, I felt myself being pulled down into another body. I could feel the modern me going into a new body like putting on a set of clothes. The sensation of being immersed deeper but awakening at the same time shocked me into alertness.

I noticed the smells first - leather, horses, hay and animal manure. My vision opened and I sat in a chair against a building. In front of me lay an open courtyard with one-story cement buildings. A log wall surrounded all the buildings. Black horses were in a corral off to my left. Most stood quietly, a few of the horses pranced around snorting. Off to the right were men wearing red tunics. Some were donning armor with shinning metal breastplates and helmets that covered their ears. 'Roman cavalry,' I thought. Many other soldiers were sitting under the eaves hand-carving what appeared to be wooden statues. I felt very relaxed and content and I just knew that I was the same person or consciousness that I had dreamt of two years ago. I am again, a Roman Centurion. Visions and warm feelings of a beautiful woman with black hair crowned with white flowers flowed through me. She is stunning. I see his memories of her; the two holding hands, talking, and laughing, hugging and kissing. I recognized the giddy feeling. 'Oh my gosh, I've felt this before with Ann, this guy is falling in love.'

Then it came, a jolting call sending me back to harsh reality. I heard a frantic voice talking to me. "Sir please, you must listen and understand the seriousness of the situation." I looked up and saw a young soldier wearing the sash of a courier on a horse looking down at me with pleading eyes. "Celonius, sir, we can lose the whole legion, we can lose Britannia!"

I could feel conflict within me as this centurion. I say 'I' because I'm again in this body of this Roman Centurion and now I know his name, Celonius. I knew and sensed this to be the same person that I became and who swam in the river during my first time-travel experience. I, Elliot, seemed to be sitting in the back of his head as an observer in the back seat of a car. Part of me felt very peaceful thinking of this lovely woman, while another part, the soldier part, wanted to jump up in response to this man's pleas.

"Centurion, the barbarians used treachery and attacked the legion by surprise, we're surrounded, many dead and wounded, we need your help Centurion. General Vespasian is questioning where you are and demands you come with your cavalry immediately!" I watched as Celonius shook his head to break loose of this apparent spell of contentment. He took a deep breath and squeezed his fists tightly. Another deep breath and I could feel a power push up from deep within him and push away the romantic feeling for this woman. Celonius then spoke with an authority and confidence I've never felt before. "Courier, dismount and show me the map with the location of the legion and the enemy." The young soldier dismounted and started to unroll a scroll that he slid out of a leather tube-like pouch. "Yes sir," he said as he opened the scroll, which I could now see was a map.

Celonius turned to a man standing behind him, "Marius, summon all the officers to come here immediately," he commanded in a stern and deliberate voice. In a snap, Marius did an about-face and ran toward the corral. The young soldier finished unrolling the scroll and stood in front of me, holding the map at chest level and at a slight angle up so that looking out through Celonius' eyes, I could easily read it. As my mind became more alert, I studied the map. A new sensation began to take hold of me, I felt myself being less Elliot, and more Celonius. But I needed to maintain my identity, to remember all that unfolded before me. Clues to archeological treasures of unimaginable wealth were at stake. I had walked into the other movie, another reality of the quantum cinema that Doctor Duningham spoke about. I had to maintain some sort of hold on my twenty first century reality. So, there were two of us in one body, Celonius the warrior, doer and main character, and Elliot, the observer sitting in the back of his consciousness, diligently observing the unfolding story.

Then it came, a sickening pain. Celonius' mind and gut churned between anger and sorrow. He thought so aloud, it was like he shouted at me, 'Betrayer! Deceiver! She led me to believe we were in love. She lied to me about peace and love for all. I should have sent out scouts. I should have caught this treason. I will make her pay for what she did no matter how fair and beautiful she is. Priestess she is not, she is a harlot."

I fought hard to stay as the observer and will only say 'I' as the narrator when it is Elliot talking. I will speak of Celonius in the third person, so you can see the story unfold as I see it.

Celonius rocked in agony within himself and I recognized his heart piercing pain, the pain a man feels when the woman he loves betrays him. His military mind took over and I felt a surge of powerful masculinity flare within him; with a military mind, he starred down at the map. The features and terrain looked vaguely similar to the map I studied in my hotel room: the hill, the fort and the plains were remarkably like the terrain I had walked this afternoon.

"Sir, you summoned us," Celonius turned to four solidly built men standing on his right. They radiated confidence and hardness of battle-tested soldiers who have fought together. More importantly, their eyes shown with admiration at being summoned to Celonius's presence which quickly shifted to a sense of concern due to the presence of the distressed courier from the Legion.

"This courier brings alarming news, it looks like thousands of Celt warriors have attacked and nearly over-run the legion. Courier, show us the tactical situation on the map." The courier pointed to a box symbol, "here is the legion's last position and the locations of the Celt's army all about 8 miles to the southeast of your location. Notice how they are massed encircling almost the entire legion. The legion has its back against this ridgeline. They're protected in the rear somewhat but also trapped. It is only a matter of time for the enemy to crest these heights and completely encircle us."

"Sir," one of the officers responded, "this doesn't make sense. The Celts, their priestess specifically as well as the elders, said peace would prevail not only in their village just south of here but in all the villages in this land, there would be no more fighting." "She deceived us, that harlot, and she will pay for her seductive evil ways," Celonius responded. He turned to the courier, "Courier, how could the legion, one of the Emperor's best, allow itself to be defeated by these peasants?"

"Sir, we camped here for just a few days to regroup before we continued our march west. The village is to the Legion's north east," he pointed to the village, "this one here, at the foot of this old hill fort. The Celts call it 'Bradene.' They must have harbored hundreds of the enemy in their huts and dwellings. From what we could ascertain, enemy insurgents must have sneaked in over two or three nights and hid in the village before they attacked. We stopped searching the village because all was peaceful. They rushed out, broke our lines of communications, killed our sentries and lookouts at the hill fort. They did this in concert with the main Celt attack. We had no warning sir. This village, sir, swore allegiance to the Emperor and they would live in peace then they took in these insurgents; we were betrayed." A hint of desperation fluttered in his voice. "The Celt first wave overran our outer perimeter and lookouts on the high grounds to our south and east. They killed most of our men," the courier hesitated as if grasping the enormity of attack and perhaps reflecting on the death of his comrades.

"They came in early morning, took us by surprise, no warning sir, many men were run through as they stepped out of their tents. My unit, the entire Rubicon cohort is gone, sir, wiped out. It was awful," his voice cracked with emotion and regardless of his strict discipline and training, the courier's body convulsed with a rush of grief over lost comrades. In an unwritten but sacred code of men, the officers lowered their heads partly in respect for their fallen comrades and partly to give this man the privacy to grieve openly without shame. Celonius put his hand on the man's heaving shoulder providing him with a measure of comfort and strength. In a moment the courier regained his composure.

"The General called for a retreat to here," he pointed to an area on the map. The officers gathered closer now as they were drawn deeper into the battle scenario and the position of the legion and the surrounding Celts. "Higher terrain, a good place to regroup. The Celts attacked and attacked again. They dented our lines but our archers got their range, sir and stung them bad, pushed back their attacks, sir. You should have a seen our archers, sir," he paused, his attitude changed to confidence while trying somehow to show joy at the destruction of the first enemy line of attack, "cut them down by the hundreds, yes sir, our archers, rained a storm of arrows on them, sir." Then his energy ebbed and he became quiet again, "But now their archers have got our range," he lowered his head and proceeded in a low voice, "Its raining arrows on us continually, men are living under their shields, many wounded, Sir, there's no food left." He gave Celonius the map and then took the reins of his horse in his hand. In a voice mixed with guilt and resolve, "I can't stay here; I've got to go back, Sir."

Still being an observer in the back of his mind, I could sense a counter attack plan being formulated. Celonius looked the man directly in the eyes; "You've done well. Ride back and tell General Vespasian to counter attack when he hears our battle horn sound twice. Do you understand? We will divert the enemy but he must rally for all of us to deal the final blow. Listen for two calls from our battle horn, then counter attack; now go!"

The young soldier, snapped to attention and raised his right arm straight out with his palm down, the Roman salute.

Firmness and resolved rippled through his entire being. He mounted his horse, kicked forward and let the horse charge toward the compound's wooden gate, which the sentries barely had time to open as he rode through at a full gallop.

Celonius turned to his officers and opened the map; "We'll follow this road to the village but break off three hundred paces from the battle front. The Celts are not fools; they are tricky, deceitful as well as masters of laying a trap. They'll be expecting us to attack to help the legion and will be waiting for us. But we will not attack them." Revenge filled his heart, his being, I could feel it and then he said, "I will make her pay, I will kill the things she loves." Emotion coursed through Celonius. "Sir?" the officers queried together.

Celonius responded, "We need to draw them out into the open and give the legion room to counter attack. We'll attack the village instead; kill everyone and everything, women, children, cows, pigs, horses. Slaughter the bastards for what they did. Then burn the place to the ground." A sharp edge of revenge came up through Celonius' body and I could feel his satisfaction flow into me for coming up with this plan. "Kill everyone and everything, but not that harlot priestess. Let her live so she can feel the pain of her lies."

But I, as Elliot, watching and hearing this plan felt revulsion. 'My God, kill everyone, innocent women, children! What's going on here?' I wanted to scream out, 'No! No! Not women and children, my God are we savages?' With effort, I held my revulsion in check for as an archeologist, I realized, 'I am an observer. Watch history unfold, I cannot and should not change anything.'

"Good sir," another officer blurted out with enthusiasm. "Yes, they'll never expect this and then they'll break ranks to protect the village," a second officer said. "Right, they'll run across this field here," he said pointing to a flat terrain area on the map, "just south of the village, then we've got them, in an open field, running out of formation, no command structure, then we've really got them," he clenched his fist tightly and struck it down like a hammer blow. His armor ruffled and clanked with the swing of his arm.

"Precisely," Celonius said, "as we attack and burn the village, the Celt army will run to defend them. That's when we reform a battle line at the south edge of the village. Before we attack from the north, we'll blow our battle horn twice signaling General Vespasian to leave his position and counter attack from the south; the legion will hit them in the rear and we will crush them on both sides." The words flowed out of our mouth like water flowing in a fast moving creek, smooth and with purpose. I say 'our' mouth for more and more I was taking on the role of Celonius. I struggled to maintain my autonomy.

Celonius then methodically gave each officer the position that their units would assume for the attack. They asked a few basic questions as to maneuvering into position, timing and reserve troops. Celonius said, "No reserves, we all go in. We'll be greatly outnumbered nearly ten to one but we'll hit them hard and fast." He repeated to assure no ambiguity in his orders, "slaughter everyone in the village and as the Celts charge out to save them, the legion will rally, hit them from the rear. We will squash them like a bug between two rocks. Go back to your units and prepare them for battle, we must leave immediately." The men presented Celonius with the Roman salute, turned sharply and double timed back to the barracks.

Alone with Celonius, who stood there clenching his fists, I could feel his anger come under control. 'She will pay for this, we'll kill everyone in that Village Bradene, then ride back here and destroy her Village Bryne killing everyone and everything.' My revulsion at killing children got the best of me. I, defying scientific protocol, called out loud, "Spare the women and children, let them live. You're a soldier; fight those who would oppose the Emperor not women and babies." Celonius raised his hands to his ears covering them, "I hear voices in my head. Am I going mad? What evil spell has come over me? I must fight this, I must stay in control." He clenched his fists again, "Quiet, this demon inside of me. I command you to be silent."

CHAPTER 17
Rebellion in the Ranks

Celonius started to breath heavily and I could feel his body shaking. He raised his hands and held his head, "I must stay in control. This witch has placed voices in my head telling me not to fight. To think, I actually loved her. Oh by the gods, what treachery this beautiful harlot has laid upon me." 'Damn it,' I thought, 'there's a lot going on here I don't know about. Who is this woman he's talking about? And, I need to shut up and not impose my feelings regardless of his order to kill woman and children. I'm starting to influence him. I must be quiet and see what will happen.' "Sir, sir," Celonius turned and his officers stood there. I could see distressed looks on their faces.

"I ask you my officers, do you understand the urgency here, do you and your men realize the situation? The legion can be destroyed while we sit here and carve statues." Celonius' voice became tense and clear. "Why are you not preparing your men and horses?" The taller man stepped forward, his face stern but his eyes dimmed with confusion, "We know what has to be done, Sir, but I have two men who refuse to fight. They say we should treat the Celts peacefully and give their land back". A second officer stepped forward, and reported, "I also have two men who said the same sir. They refuse to fight."

Celonius looked at the other officers. I could feel his confusion, his feeling of loss of control and an ever-growing pain. The pain and weakness over this elegant woman, who has betrayed him, confounded by being jolted out of the peace that his battle weary soul needed, mobilizing to wage war in this emergency and now, a rebellion among his men.

"Rebellion in the ranks, this is treason, it's a plot woven by the Celts", his voice slowed to a near whisper, "that witch harlot." The pain racked deeper through him as the image of a beautiful woman he thought of so tenderly, her smiling face flashed in front of me. Her large soft green eyes, flowing black hair, radiated a glow of femininity that fluttered right through me. In an instant I fell in love with her, wanted her, needed her and then, I realized that again somehow, I knew her. His panic raced through me, a sense of total loss, an agony beyond description coursed through us. To be betrayed by this woman, this ethereal goddess crushed any sense of valor or manhood that we had. In a terrifying instant, I realized the ultimate power a woman can have over a man.

But as a storm passes and quiet comes, this pain leaves us. I felt Celonius grasping again for his authority. I could see him recalling moments of battle, the slaying of fierce enemies, the glory of the Emperor rewarding his valor. Pride and strength flowed back into him on a tidal wave of courage.

He stepped forward, stood tall, regained his composure, and spoke with renewed power, "And you Lanius, Marcus, speak up, do you have traitors in your ranks too?" His surge of energy quickly received another hammer blow. Marcus stepped forward, "Celonius, two of my best men, Titus and Pilatus, seasoned veterans, said they will fight no more."

Dread flowed back into Celonius. 'Not Titus. No, not him!' he thought. Like an observer high on a rampart looking down and watching scenes unfold, visions of Titus fighting side by side with Celonius flashed in front of me. A profound sense of loss, a loss of comrades in arms, turned into nausea. 'How much can this guy take,' I wondered. Compassion for this battered man overwhelmed me. I admired his drive to regain composure despite the crisis that continued to overshadow him. I could be quiet no longer, "You can do it Celonius, you are a great leader, be strong, these men need you now more than ever and they will follow you." I said this without regret at breaking any directives of non-interference. I spoke to him man to man and began to feel deep admiration for him. Here was a man, bigger than life, a hero of history, facing more challenges of leadership in a few minutes than I would face in a lifetime.

It worked, Celonius's hunched body, stood upright like a tower reaching into the sky, his muscles flexed solid, his hand gripped the pummel of his sword and he stood there, a powerful warrior. He pointed to the last officer, "Speak."

Linius spoke, "Seems, sir, I've been hit the hardest, five men also refuse to fight. Each laid down their Gladius and said we should try to live in peace and not fight the Celts."

"Have you reasoned with them; tried to talk them out of their position?" Celonius asked. Concern for his men started to overshadow his warrior fierceness. "Sir, we've taken them aside to talk but they openly refused to change their minds," Marcus said. He paused and then looked pleadingly at Celonius, "They proclaimed their refusal to fight in front of the other men, sir. We've never faced anything like this before, since Rome, since Gaul, we've all fought together. The other men are torn, sir, there's mumbling about not fighting anymore, we've got to do something." A pang of confusion and regret surged through him. This had never happened to any Roman commander. Celonius fought back the confusion and like a martial artist using the force of an opponent to flip him to the ground, I could feel the confusion turn into the power of resolve.

"Assemble the men in battle formation, here in the assembly area. Now!" He pointed to the open football field sized area behind where we stood. "Bring the dissenters out and line them up in front." Celonius barked out these orders in a heavy rough command. The men saluted and left to carry out their orders.

'What is he going to do?' I thought. I felt curiosity about what my hero had planned. 'He is a wise and courageous man. Whatever it is, somehow, I know it will be the right thing.' Little did I know I would be in for the most terrifying event in my life.

Celonius pondered, 'I will talk to them, appeal to their loyalty as soldiers of the Emperor. We need to fight now, I will discipline them later.' 'But what if they still say no?' a thought came from deep within him. 'What is your alternate plan? You always have another option, you need one here, too!'

The officers called their men into formation in the field. They lined up in perfect columns and rows in full cavalry riding uniform. They made an impressive and fearful scene wearing shinning metal breastplates and helmets, leather armor, dark red riding pants down to their knees, bare calves and leather footwear. They stood stoically like living statues in an outdoor museum. A Hollywood movie with all its special effects could not rival this scene. With their horses still in a corral, a full cohort of Roman cavalry stood before me; they echoed the real might of Roman rule that anyone living in the twenty first century could only read about. The spectacle of all that armor reflecting the sunlight caused my eyes to squint from the glare. Elliot, the archeologist, needed to stay aware. I started taking mental notes about their uniforms, the buildings, equipment, the horses and how they were harnessed. I beheld an archeologist's dream come true. I stood in the middle of an event where 2000 years from this time I would dig for what I'm observing right now.

The dissenters marched in a line and stopped about ten feet in front of the troops. I could feel more resolve spread through

Celonius but hidden deep inside him were insecurities that silently gnawed away at him, 'What if they say, NO?'

"I give you men one last chance to renounce your decision not to fight for the Empire. You will be punished or you may rejoin the troop as a critical battle lay before us. What say you? Will you be men of the Empire or traitors to your country?" His voice bellowed loudly assuring the last man in the last rank could hear clearly. I could feel his hand reach down and pull out his sword. The classic sound of raw steel being unleashed from its scabbard echoed against this audience of armored men. The Gladius, the Roman battle sword, felt good and balanced in my hand. I could feel the power it gave me. There's something about a primal weapon like a sword. Unlike a modern firearm, which derives its power from its technology, the sword derives its power from the person who holds it. The sword becomes an extension of the person; his balance, grace and strength extend from his body and into the sword. I felt this now and with it I noticed an even more dramatic occurrence.

Like a person standing on a ledge senses he is losing his balance, my Elliot identity was about to fall completely from me. I knew in a moment I would be totally absorbed into Celonius. No longer a curious observer in the back of his mind, I sensed my plunge forward into his frontal lobe. I shot forward into the foreground of Celonius' mind and became one with his thinking process.

'Bastards, they force me to do this, I must, I must act now or the others will mutiny.' I could now hear and speak these words. I raised my sword high so all could see it. "Swear allegiance to the Emperor or you die!" I screamed as I walked behind them. Silence pervaded everything. Even the herd of horses in their corral became dead quiet like an audience watching an intense part of a play. Stillness surrounded everything. Behind me the soldiers stood as solid as ice but the traitors stood steadfast. Not a one said a word of regret.

Rage filled my body like electricity as I screamed, "Can't you see, you're under the witches spell? It's all part of their plan. They attacked the legion by treachery; they do the same to us now." Desperation flowed through me. I didn't want to do this. I raised my gladius even higher and screamed, "Fellow soldiers of the Emperor, your last chance. Swear your allegiance."

Stillness, silence, deafening silence.

I felt the sweet cool balance of the sword as I raised it back. Everything slowed down, as if in slow motion and my mind reached out to run from what was about to happen. No longer wanting to participate in this, a tiny fragment of Elliot fought to run away and go back to being an archeologist. But the balanced momentum of the Gladius exhilarated me. My mind clung to this sensation, 'well designed this weapon, the ideal thrusting sword for a straight out strike and kill. Well done you engineers and artisans of death who made this blade.'

I screamed, what I don't know, with all the power within me. The sword shot forward guided by the powerful muscles in my arms right into the back of Titus, my once trusted sergeant. I heard the deadly puncture of flesh failing to resist the plunge of sharp cold steel. Blood shot out immediately from his muscular back. I felt resistance as the blade cut through his body and move faster as it passed through into clear air stopping abruptly as the hilt jammed into his back. I held it there until his body went limp. It took awhile, for Titus, despite his desire for peace still possessed the muscles of a soldier. His body stood tense, then convulsed for a second or so. Blood trickled from his mouth. Tension left his once strong muscles and his body fell to the ground.

Everything started to spin and I fell into a pit of darkness, I recognized the sensation, I started to travel counterclockwise forward in time again, I felt totally helpless, scared. Thankfully, the vertigo like journey ended. I opened my eyes to my small hotel room with the old wood dresser, the mirror hung crookedly on the wall, my suitcase, the map at the side of the bed, my clothes thrown over the end chair.

I didn't have time to notice the sweat pouring off of me nor how my bed sheets were soaked with sweat. The scene of a dying man spitting blood with his convulsing body at the end of a sword that I had thrust through him seared my mind and body. The scene of on-looking soldiers, cold and stoic but with a wince of pain and sadness in their eyes as a trusted comrade betrayed them and was executed made me feel their pain.

Then it came, in my stomach, revulsion, of what I had done. I had never hurt anyone before except on the football field in undergrad school and now I had just slaughtered a man who was my compatriot. I needed to vomit.

Physically and emotionally sick, I ran for the bathroom crashing into the door, pushing it open, losing my balance, falling onto the shower curtain and then into the tub. Somehow I got up without puking all over myself and dove for the toilet, raising the lid just in time.

I hugged the bowl as a drowning man hugs a life preserver while my stomach wretched out its contents. The room spun and the toilet became my only hold on reality. In a moment of brief consciousness, I remembered that Charles had the room right next to mine. I reached up and pounded on the bathroom wall with my fist in desperation. I needed help.

The pounding worked and I could hear Charles banging on my door. Half conscious with no energy left, I fell limp onto the bathroom floor. Off in the distance, I could hear what sounded like the jingling of keys and Charles' voice calling out. In the moment I was falling onto the floor, he summoned the night clerk. Good old Charles, like a mother hen, he was looking after his young American chick. I remember being picked up under both arms and carried back to bed. "These Yanks could never hold their liquor, ehh Professor?" the desk clerk said. "Nonsense, this man didn't drink at all, I've been with him all night," Charles replied.

"Charles, I killed him. My God, I killed him in cold blood," my voice cracked as my shaking clammy hand reached up and clutched his arm. Waves of remorse and guilt flooded through me, my body started to fall into shock. "Oh, my!" said the desk clerk raising his hand to his mouth in surprise. "He's killed someone." He stepped back in horror. "Killed someone in the hotel?" Charles responded immediately. "He's hallucinating, don't mind him, I'm a doctor, and he's under my care," Charles said firmly just as a doctor would give orders to a nurse. "Raise his feet up and put this blanket over him."

Charles leaned over me, "Take deep slow breaths Elliot. That's it, deep and slow breaths. You'll be fine." I did what he directed and the panic and weakness that had drained me was replaced by a sense of calm. Charles looked sternly at the clerk and nodded toward the door. "You can leave now, thank you, and I'll take it from here. Go on now, I have work to do here, and thank you for your help." "Er, eh, yes, doctor, if you need any more help, I'll be down at the desk. Do you need me to call an ambulance?"

Showing just a bit of firmness and gratitude, a trait he must have developed by working for decades with well meaning but slightly incompetent archeology students, Charles replied, "That's very kind of you, I'll consider that but I believe all will be fine, if I may spend a few moments with my patient who very much needs my attention, please leave. Now!" With that brisk remark, the desk clerk dashed out.

"Elliot. Relax, keep breathing slowly and deeply, all is well, you're safe now." His confidence and reassuring speech gently coaxed me back to this reality. With Charles' help I sat up in my bed, took a few more deep breaths and felt my consciousness totally return. My vision cleared and oddly, I felt somewhat at peace, like one would feel after a deep profound sleep.

Charles, seeing color come back to my face asked, "Now Elliot, what happened? What do you mean you 'killed him'? Did you travel back again?"

CHAPTER 18
Return to the Present

"Yes, big time, really big time, Charles," I said letting out a deep breath. "Better get a pad and pen and take notes before some details leave me," I said pointing to the table where my books and sketchpads were laying. I relayed the entire story to Charles. He asked questions, many questions that an archeologist and historian would ask. The type of saddles on the horses, the difference in amour that the officers and soldiers wore, weapons, lances, the differences in uniform colors, type of building construction I may have noticed. Like a district attorney methodically questioning a witness, Charles asked questions that developed a picture of general life in the cavalry cohort of Legion II Augusta.

I cooperated fully, pausing to answer his questions, closing my eyes to re-visit the scenes. I started to feel the anger and confusion of Celonius as he decided to execute the traitors. Not wanting to face what I saw or did, I buried my face in my hands and started to recall the details. As I told him of those brave men who wanted peace and decided not to fight, how they marched out solemn in their conviction, and how Celonius or I killed Titus, I felt the nausea and sorrow build up inside me again. My voice cracked, my shoulders quivered as the horror of seeing a man die at my own hand, his body going limp as his life left him.

Charles put his hand on my shoulder, "Detach yourself Elliot, I know you witnessed and experienced the brutality of an execution but remember, 'It wasn't you. So, detach yourself from it. Remember it's just a movie, a bloody powerful movie but you're in the audience. Right?" "Wrong, Charles," I countered, looking up at him, tears filling my eyes and with a challenge in my wavering voice, "Wrong, I wasn't in any damn audience, I'm in this guy's head. No, I am him, this Roman Centurion. I feel his power, his pride but also his fear and confusion. I see out through his eyes, feel with his hands, walk with his feet, and talk through his mouth, damn hard to be an audience in that position."

I didn't want to be cross with Charles as he could provide my only way out of this emotional mess. My hands trembled and within seconds of sobbing, I could feel my emotional control slipping away. Scared, confused, sick and overcome with guilt and remorse for executing a man I put my face back in my hands as I sat upright in my bed. Charles sat down on the bed next to me and lowered his head. "Sorry, Elliot, you've suffered much in such an incredible experience. But, look at it this way, you've advanced Roman archeology in England, hundreds of years forward. We know facts now that we could never have dreamed and you are paying the price for it. How can I help you? Do you have any insight into why it happened tonight?"

I slowed my thinking trying to remember the exact details that led to my time shift. "I reviewed the maps before I went to sleep. Yes, the maps of the area. My vision started by reading the maps the courier from the legion showed me and Celonius." I forced myself to remember the maps I saw in the vision, "And they were of the same area as the maps we're using now. Maybe that's what triggered the memory and the plunge back in time?" Charles reached down and picked up the maps that had fallen to the floor. He laid them out before me and said, "Point to the areas that look familiar, I mean that were the same in the vision you had."

I looked down and searched for key landmarks. "Well, while the Romans excelled in cartography, the detail in these modern maps far outstrip those Roman maps," I said. I studied the map further, looking for familiar landmarks. "Here's the site we visited today, the hill with its descending ridge line to the south. The attack took place eight miles to the southwest at a hill-fort. Here, right here," my finger jabbed the map. I saw the tell-tale valley that the legion had been pushed back into with the high hills covering their rear, the area that the Celts attacked from and the attack path drawn out by Celonius to his officers. I pointed these landmarks out to Charles. "This is where the legion had camped and the Celts infiltrated into this village and overran the Romans in a morning sneak attack," I said as I ran my finger over the battle area. "South Cadbury?" asked Charles.

I checked the map again, "That's right, Celonius wanted to destroy the whole town, kill everyone for harboring the Celts that overpowered the Roman sentries." "You know what that means my psychic American friend?" Charles asked. "Yes, my fine British mentor, right here," I pointed just to the southwest of the South Cadbury Hillfort, "is where we can find the remnants of that ancient Celtic village." "Well, Elliot, as you Yanks say, you just 'drove one out of the park,' again." He stood up and smiled, "Get some rest, you need to sleep this out and balance your mind. See you for breakfast."

I slept well, my past life vision so tired me that after Charles left, I fell into a deep calm sleep. I awoke early and went for a jog, my mind clear, and ready for our meeting with the Gilcrists. I ran through the narrow streets, no more than a car width wide. The entrances to old brick homes opened right onto the street. If a resident opened a front door while a car drove by, there would be an embarrassing collision. I wondered how often this happened. I showered when I got back to my room and met Charles for breakfast in a small restaurant across from the hotel. Charles sitting in a corner booth smiled as I, full of confidence and smiling, sat down across from him. After a sip of tea he said, "I spoke to my assistant, Mrs. Grieves back on campus, she's mobilizing a team to come out here by the weekend to start the dig. I've closed down two minor sites we're currently working. This site here, the possible chapel of Brother Leonidas is like the holy grail of dig sites. We do need to start as soon as possible," he paused for a moment, sipped some tea and looked at me somewhat apologetically. "Sorry old chap for getting down to business first thing, how are you after last night?"

"Never thought you'd ask," I said between gulps of coffee, "I'm fine, slept like a baby, dreamt of Rebecca and that's nice." "A remarkably intelligent woman, just about your age too," Charles commented. "She does set off the arousal alarm inside of me. In fact, I remember now that I'd been thinking about her when I examined the maps last night before I had that past life regression," I paused. "I believe that's what it's officially called. And you know Charles, somehow she reminds me of the woman Celonius was fantasizing over in my time travel session last night." "Notice that both times you've had these experiences, you've been with a woman?" Charles said just before he took a bite of his scrambled eggs.

"Strange, maybe they're a part of my past life or parallel reality," I replied. I called the waitress over for more coffee.

CHAPTER 19
Rebecca & Anna

"I couldn't sleep last night," Rebecca said to her mother as they cleaned up after breakfast. The men had either gone into the fields to work or into town on business. "Was it caused by the American?" Anna asked. Her motherly intuition knew that her daughter's normal 'in control' demeanor seemed shaken since their meeting the other day with the archeology team. "Yes, I've been haunted by him. How did you know?" Rebecca asked somewhat perplexed.

"I'm your mother Rebecca, I know these things," she replied. "Tell me more about what you're feeling dearest daughter." Anna Gilcrist smiled at this unique chance of sharing feelings with her business like 'always in control' daughter.

"Mother, there's something alluring about him. I feel I've known him before, known him very well," Rebecca said as she put away a stack of dishes in the overhead cupboard. "I'm nervous when I'm with him but also sense some sort of power and attachment to him. My God, I've only been with him for a few hours and I feel like a young school girl,"

Rebecca leaned up against the kitchen counter, folded her arms and puffed air in a narrow stream, blowing strands of long dangling hair that fell across her face. "I can't believe this is happening to me," she said. Anna put her hand softly on Rebecca's shoulder, "Sounds deeper than infatuation my dear. Perhaps a past life together?" Rebecca looked perplexed then shrugged her shoulders, "Maybe, that just may be. You know that I have run across countless men in my career. Some are quite handsome and dynamic." Rebecca raised her right hand, "But none have even come close to casting a spell on me like this American archeologist, Elliot. What should I do mother, I'm not being rational about this."

"You're a woman my dear and God has given you wonderful instincts. They will come to you automatically if you let them. Put your rational mind aside for a while. Meditate and become more in touch with your soul. Follow your instincts, you will be guided." Anna's hand slid down Rebecca's back and she pulled her reluctant daughter's body toward hers. She embraced Rebecca softly giving her the warmth of her energy. "Thank you mother, thank you." Rebecca raised her arms and hugged her mother tightly. She dropped her head onto Anna's shoulder and for a wonderful brief moment, Rebecca became a little girl again. Anna rocked her slowly and gently for a magical moment.

Rebecca stood erect returning to adulthood. "Elliot and Dr. Weldon will be here in an hour what if they ask questions, not only about the hill but about all of our land. What about the mysteries you spoke about yesterday morning?" Rebecca asked. Her mother sighed, "Like I said, times are changing and much will be revealed in the coming week. Let's leave it to the Divine. But, my busy minded daughter, remember what I said, feel your intuition, meditate in stillness, like you do in yoga, let your soul talk to you." Rebecca smiled and hugged her mother briefly again. "Thank you mother." She turned to leave but then stopped, turned back to Anna and embraced her tightly. "Hold me again mother, tightly." The morning light streamed through the kitchen window and onto the two women in their tender loving embrace.

CHAPTER 20
First Meeting at the Manor

"Now that I've just about mastered driving on the wrong side of the road, you want to drive," I said to Charles as he motioned me to sit in the passenger's seat. "Did you say the 'wrong side'," Charles replied as he fastened his seat belt. He slid his seat to a comfortable position, adjusted the rear view mirror and reached outside and turned the side mirror slightly outward.

"Charles, there are more cars in my home town of New York than there are in all of England and probably 50 times more cars in the US than in the UK. All those drivers can't be 'wrong' besides Henry Ford was an American," I said sinking back into my seat. "Really," Charles said as he looked at me. "Good try, but I'm not convinced, besides quantity doesn't mean quality." He pulled out onto the road and accelerated shifting through the gears like he was driving at Daytona. "Way to go Charles," I said, "what happened to that conservative English professor?"

We drove up to the Gilcrist manor turning off the main road onto a long drive marked by weathered stone pillars. The manor lay before us at the end of a wide paved driveway a few hundred yards long and wide enough for two cars. Giant oak trees spaced about fifty feet apart lined the entire length of the drive. Their overhanging branches forming a natural shaded canopy. I opened up my window and stuck my head out to get a better view. The matrix of branches, green leaves with occasional patches of sunlight streaking through created a display of dazzling light, shade and colors. At the perimeter of neighboring trees, branches often interlocked forming triangles, arcs and various intersecting angles. The patterns made a natural fresco that flowed like a Tchaikovsky symphony.

"You're not going to jump are you? I didn't think my driving was that bad," Charles said as I extended my body half out of the window. I pulled my head back in. "The show is up above us, beautiful array of branches, leaves, shadows and light. Go ahead and try it." I stuck my head back outside and felt the car coming to a stop. "Michelangelo could not have sculptured a more dramatic masterpiece," I said. Charles stuck his head out and for that one moment we both gazed up and shared the natural wonder above us. "Took hundreds of years to make this," he said, "and too bad people can't learn how to cooperate and get along like these trees. Marvelous, simply marvelous!" "Marvelous," I said, "But not natural, more like supernatural, eh?"

Both of us sat back in our seats and finished the drive up to the manor. I guess you can say that the Gilcrists seem to live in a typical English Manor, like you see in the movies. Old red brick structure complete with statues of lions, gargoyles, and bricked walkways meandering through well-kept gardens. A long single story garage stood off to our left, overhead doors covering the sleeping cars within. Based on the richness of the manor, I imagined a Bentley, Rolls Royce or a Ferrari sitting in the garage.

Charles and I walked toward the main entrance door, it opened and Robin stepped out. "Welcome to Gilcrist, gentlemen, one of the oldest manors in the county," he said extending his hand and gave us a sincere hardy handshake. We entered and he gave us a quick tour of the downstairs rooms. True to classic manor form, knights in armor stood in each room, tapestry of woodlands and hunting scenes hung on the walls while heavy wood furniture populated each room. Charles looked around with silent awe. The rooms also had large clear and stained glass windows allowing an abundance of natural light to cascade in. Even more impressive, the placement of the stained glass allowed their colored light to blend with the light passing through the clear glass windows and, like different instruments in a symphony orchestra, harmonized together to make a mosaic of light and colors. Each room used a different color scheme offering a relaxing but rejuvenating atmosphere.

I mentioned this color phenomenon to Robin. "The color sequence changes as the sun travels across the sky. And to add to it all, since the sun travels angularly in its seasonal changes, it is really never in the same exact place at the same time the following day, the color patterns change daily and repeat each other only once every year," Robin said with a sense of genuine pride.

I realized that the Gilcrist's possessed a unique relationship with nature. The tunnel of trees with their geometrical patterns and now the unique sunlight patterns that change every day showed me they used nature to enhance the beauty of their home. "Robin, your family has a unique relationship with nature," I said as we walked down a sunlit hallway. Robin replied, "stop and look at the floor in this hallway, it appears to be mosaic doesn't it?" I looked down at the floor colored like a stained glass window with patterns of green, ruby, violet, yellow and blue. Instead of the pattern of glass mosaic on a window, it radiated within the floor. "Nice," Charles said, "it looks like it was laid yesterday, good craftsmanship."

Like a sheepish boy who just pulled a prank on his parents, Robin smiled and said, "Go ahead and touch it." Charles and I stood before the mosaic hallway that stretched before us leading to a large room where I heard female voices. I felt a stirring in me hoping that one of the voices I heard was Rebecca's. I felt like a teenager again waiting to see his first girlfriend. "Go ahead," Robin said, "see what it's made off." Bending down, Charles reached out to touch the floor. A shadow the shape of his arm and hand appeared on the floor. "What the…." Charles said. I laid my palm flat on the floor directly on a green and violet mosaic pattern. The top of my hand turned the color of the pattern. "The color doesn't come from the floor," I said. I looked up and saw a stained glass window high in the ceiling above me. Charles looked up at the same time, "By Jove, it's coming from that colored skylight. But it looks like mosaic tile on the floor. Truly amazing."

Robin bent down next to us, "Yes, quite a trick of the eye isn't it?" He put his hand on the walkway floor and instantly the color pattern of yellow and blue appeared on his hand. "Feel the texture of the floor itself." Charles and I dutifully ran our hands over the floor. The color patterns from the overhead skylight danced on our hands and forearms changing colors as a chameleon changes color walking over different colored leaves. "The texture seems porous," I said, "not too smooth but not too rough either." "Right," Robin said, "the floor is a fine concrete, it possesses just the right texture to capture the light and radiate it back just enough to make it appear that the color is embedded in the floor itself." He raised his hand, palm open, emphasizing that the color streams down from the skylight above. "Does it change as the sun moves?" Charles asked.

"One would think that," Robin replied, "but the angle or convexity, the outward bulge of the skylight above captures the sun light for about four hours and directs it to this very area of the walkway." "All year?" I asked. "Four hours in the summer, three in the winter when the sun is lower in the sky," he replied. "Amazing, absolutely amazing," Charles said, "You must give me the name of the contractors or architect you used to do this. I know just the place in my humble home where I would have this built." "Sorry I can't do that Dr. Weldon," Robin said. Charles looked dejected, "Why not?" "The men who designed and crafted all of this died over 400 years ago," Robin said. Standing up, Robin moved his arm directing us to the room at the end of the walkway.

As we entered a classically furnished English study, a majestic Persian rug lay in the center of the room with a wood and glass table in its center. High back dark leather chairs encircled it. The layout reminded me of an ancient meeting site with stone seats circling a fire pit. Perhaps, considering the age and symbolism embedded in what I saw of their manor, the Gilcrists designed the room to resemble an ancient gathering place. Two ladies sat to our right. Rebecca smiled when we walked in. She looked as lovely as the day before. Her straight black hair, green eyes, tender face and shapely but strong body radiated healthy confidence coupled with an assured manner.

Mrs. Gilcrist, smaller but as equally elegant as Rebecca, had short silver blonde hair, she looked much younger than I expected her to be. She dressed casually but displayed an air of properness about her with meticulously styled hair, smart color coordinated jewelry, obviously an inherited necklace, ring and earrings. Her jewelry reflected a Celtic design. She rose to greet us and stood like a lioness poised in front of her pride. No doubt existed in my mind of who ran the manor.

After brief introductions in which Charles displayed his usual British etiquette while I easily fell into the role of the casual American. Mrs. Gilcrist got right down to business. She relayed quite politely but emphatically that the Gilcrists were a private family; the manor and its surrounding fields and hills had been in the family for over a millennia. They appreciated and understood the value of living with and in nature; they respected every square inch of their blessed land and wanted to make one specific request.

"We welcome your archeology team on our land because we appreciate the historic significance that may exist at the site. But under no circumstances shall you or any of your group stray from the hilltop or explore any other part of the farm. Further, news media is strictly forbidden, all documentation and photography shall be in a scholarly manner and under no situation shall the location of the site or the Gilcrist name be mentioned in any published reports. The location and Gilcrist name shall be kept in strictest confidence by the university under the threat of lawsuit if any of that information 'leaks out'. Am I clear on this Professor Weldon and Dr. Rizzo?"

A moment of stunned silence followed as Charles and I tried to process this demand. She looked at us like the CEO of a large corporation, expecting complete capitulation to her demands. "Mrs. Gilcrist," Charles responded with all the assuredness he could muster, "speaking for the university, I promise you we shall comply with every iota of your request and ..." But before Charles could say anymore, she put out her hand to stop him, looked sternly in his eye, "Dr. Weldon this is not a request, this is an emphatic condition for you being allowed on our land, do you understand the difference?" Charles took a deep breath and a look of regret in his eyes said, "Yes, madam, please forgive my poor choice of words, I assure you we will comply with every condition you have stated."

I sat in utter silence exchanging quick but serious glances with Rebecca. We both understood instinctively the drama that had unfolded in front of us and thought it best if we took a back seat to the proceedings. "Good," Mrs. Gilcrist responded, her attitude of authority not diminishing one bit. She took out a folder and placed it on the ornate glass and intricately carved wood coffee table in front of us. "Here's a contract drawn up by my attorney outlining everything I said, plus more. All you have to do to start your archeological work is to sign the agreement and coordinate your schedule with Rebecca and Robin. They will be the Gilcrist family liaison for your work."

I felt a surge of joy upon hearing that Rebecca would be working with us. I glanced again at her just in time to catch her eyes leaving me and turning to Charles. I felt even better when I saw her smile, which in some sort of covert feminine way I took as a signal she was happy too. "Mrs. Gilcrist, the university's legal department will have to review your document. I'll hand deliver it myself today. Is there anything else you'd like to discuss or, should I say, tell us?"

"Not really," she replied, "Do you have any questions?" Her eyes open wide waiting somewhat impatiently to answer any questions. But Charles retained his cool and like General Montgomery at the Battle of El Alamein, seemed to be strategizing a counter attack. "Well yes now that I have had a moment to consider. I'd like to have my associate start a preliminary survey of the site during a day or so while I'm at the university taking care of these legal matters," Charles asked. Mrs. Gilcrist frowned. Charles sensing the pending rejection leaned forward and taking on a more persuasive tone said, "Surely, Dr Rizzo," he turned and motioned to me, "Elliot will, as you directed, stay at the hill top site only. He'll make preliminary layouts of the site, he's very good at that." Before Mrs. Gilcrist could refuse, help came from an unexpected source.

"Mother, I think that's a fair request. Doctor Rizzo has a respected reputation in early Britannia archeology. We're fortunate to have him work on our site," Rebecca's request like the proverbial cavalry coming over the hill seemed to lighten the intense look on Mrs. Gilcrist's ever-stern face. Rebecca's voice sounded business like but I did detect a slight hint of 'please mother' echoing in the undertone of her request. More important I felt an instant bond with her. She seemed to be interested both in the archeology of the site and me as well. Artfully, she avoided looking or even glancing at me when she spoke to her mother. An attempt, I thought, to disguise her interest in me.

"Well," the older woman said, "we can do this legally if we consider this work part of the original visit. Our lawyers have already approved that." She turned to me, "Dr. Rizzo, I approve your survey work 'on the hill'. You can start immediately but digging or removing any artifacts or changing the site in any way from as it is now, is strictly forbidden. Is that clear." "Yes, ma'am," I acknowledged. She turned to Rebecca, "Rebecca dear, when is a good time for you to accompany Dr. Rizzo in starting his survey." In a seemingly slow and deliberate response, "Tomorrow morning will work just fine. I'll be free most of the day."

I glanced at Charles who sat back in his chair and just smiled. I could almost read his mind, 'Mission accomplished.'

CHAPTER 21
Rebecca's Nightmare

The next morning at 5:00 am, a woman's scream echoed through the second floor bedrooms of the ancient Gilcrist manor. Another scream, louder, vibrated further down the hall past the two armored knights, deep red tapestries, the dark wood paneled halls and rattled the large picture window. Rebecca sat up in her bed, sweating, shaking. Her mother, frantically putting on her robe ran across the hallway to Rebecca's room. Her motherly instincts and fears on full alert, she was ready to help and protect her daughter.

Rebecca's bedroom door flew open, "Rebecca dear," she said, "what in the world? Are you alright?" She sat down on the bed next to her sobbing daughter and even though Rebecca was twenty-eight years old, her mother cradled her head and placed her arm around her shaking daughter as she had done when Rebecca was a child.

Shaking, gasping for breath her body convulsing in sobs, "Oh mother, how horrible. Children were screaming and being stabbed to death, homes burning, women slaughtered, blood all over." She looked at her mother and raised her hand to grasp the older woman's shoulder. "The Romans, they killed, they butchered everyone, with a vengeance, they did it. Oh God! It was like I was there, right in the middle of it. So real, mother, so real." Her head fell into her mother's shoulder. Rebecca cried again, uncontrollably.

Robin stood in the doorway with only his shorts on. "Is she ok, mum?" Lance came up behind him, also in his shorts, his hair disheveled, "What's going on? Damn! Woke up to this scream. Is Rebecca alright, huh?" Anna Gilcrist answered, "A nightmare; she's had a terrible nightmare. Go on back to sleep while it is still dark. I'll take care of her, go on now." Rebecca's sobbing muffled by her mother's soft satin robe echoed in the background. Lance turned around immediately and stomped back toward his room shaking his head.

"Are you sure mum?" said Robin a bit more aware and concerned than his older brother. Robin and Rebecca were close. Rebecca always watched out for her younger brother. Robin hanging on to every word his sister said as she read bedtime stories to him. Those were the early days of their childhood and their bond stood firm even though now as adults they were both actively involved in their own lives.

Robin looked down at his sobbing sister by now being fully embraced and rocked like a baby by their mother. As if on cue, knowing that Robin stood there concerned about her, Rebecca, extended out her hand to him, beckoning him to come and comfort her. He grabbed her outstretched hand and sat on the bed.

"Tell me what happened sis'? What did you dream about?" he said. "This was no dream." she said, "My God, it couldn't have been more real." She sat up, leaving their embrace. She inhaled deeply, yoga style, three times to fill her depleted lungs with air and to try to calm down. Before her mother could hand her the tissue box from her night table, Rebecca reached out and took out a handful of tissues and dried her eyes, then blew her nose. She slid back a few inches toward her headboard and brought up her knees wrapping her arms around them. After a few more deep breaths, Rebecca had composed herself enough to talk.

"I had an experience, it wasn't a dream or a vision, for I was there, in the middle of a massacre," she said. She looked up into Robin's deep compassionate gaze and felt her mother's reassuring hand on her shoulder. Rebecca could not hold it back, her face furrowed, her eyes strained, she started to cry again. "Its ok, sis, it must have been horrible," he said, his voice soothing and comforting. Both he and his mother knew that the special energy of the manor, coupled with their ancient family traditions, could evoke deep emotional experiences. "Take another deep breathe, relax, you don't have to tell us anything now. It is alright, you're here with us."

"No!" Rebecca snapped, "I have to say what I saw, it's the only way I can clear it from my mind." Regaining her composure, she sat back against the headboard, with a determined and resolute air, took a deep breath, sighed, closed her eyes and spoke in a detached monotone voice. "While I slept, it happened, not more than a half hour ago, I remember spinning, spinning and falling, as if I had fallen into a tornado or some sort of vortex. I started to hear screaming, children, woman, calling out in pain, "No, No, Please stop!" Then I heard the loud yells of men, the clang of swords," Rebecca opened her eyes to see Robin and her mother intently starring at her.

"I had glimpses of woman and children running, then the scene would go back into the vortex, then return to the women and children, old people, too. Finally, I popped into the scene and then saw them, the soldiers, on jet-black horses. They wore silver breastplates and helmets. I recognized them as Romans. So I must have been somewhere nearly two thousand years ago."

Light started to come through the window in her room as the sun continued slowly upward from below the horizon. "Wait a moment, sis," Robin said, "What do you mean you 'popped' into the scene." "Yes, I was going to ask the same question," her mother said. Rebecca took another slow breath, "You know what its like when you're in plane flying in the clouds and you're coming in to land. Layers of clouds go by and you catch quick glimpses of the ground, a little here, a little ground there, and the next thing you know, you pop out of the clouds and the ground appears in full view. It was like that." She stopped, looked up at them seeking agreement and confirmation. Robin and her mother both nodded.

"Were you running with the women and children or just standing there?" "At first I just stood there but not standing there on my two feet." She closed her eyes recalling what she experienced. "I was, I was … sitting on a horse. Yes, it's coming back to me now. A horse, chestnut color, standing between the running people who are running from the attacking Romans on their black horses," she stared blankly at the wall like a prisoner staring at her cell wall, recalling these terrible acts. "But they left me alone, they rode past me. I remember yelling at them, telling them to stop, but they ignored me. They caught up to fleeing villagers and cut them down," she put her face into her hands and shook her head as if in disbelief at what she saw. "Oh God, the screaming, the blood, horses trampling children, mothers screaming, hiding their children under their cloaks. Oh yes, and the fires, the smoke, I could hardly breath," her voice trailed off into a whisper. She coughed as if clearing her lungs of some non-existent smoke. "What burned?" her mother asked.

"A village," Rebecca raised her head and looked at her mother, "Huts, large thatched huts, they burned with a piercing snapping sound like twigs or branches breaking. You know, mother, like when you break them up for kindling for our fireplace." She paused for a moment, closing her eyes to bring the events back into focus. Rebecca convulsed again as she relived the horror, "Some of the Romans on horseback would run down a fleeing woman or elder, pick them up by their hair, ride toward a burning hut and throw their captive into the fire. Oh my God, what a slaughter, such brutality." She lowered her head and sobbed again. Robin and Anna held her tighter. With resolve, she raised her head and continued, "strange, when those Romans rode by me, they looked at me, but didn't strike out at me. Although, I found it difficult to make out their facial features because of their helmets, the dust, and the speed, which they rode by me, I swear some of them looked familiar. In fact one of them, their leader, probably a Centurion, I could tell by the rigid red plume on his helmet, trotted to within a few feet of me, I could see on his face intense sorrow that turned to anger. "Did he say anything to you?" her mother asked.

Rebecca closed her eyes to concentrate. Robin put his hand on her shoulder and softly massaged her shoulder and neck. He knew that their visit to the ruins with the archeologists had something to do with this dream. Some ancient event that died to human memory two millennia ago had come back to life and reached out its bloody hand to his sister.

"Yes, yes, he did," she whispered. "He said: 'Why did you do this? I trusted you, I fell in love with you.'" She looked up at her brother and mother in disbelief, became sullen and slowly shook her head and pointed to her chest. "As if this all was my fault, he seemed to be blaming me for the massacre!" "He said he loved you. Did he look familiar to you?" Robin asked.

She closed her eyes and shook her head, "Yes, yes! I don't know how, or when or where, but yes. I felt some sort of exhilaration when I saw him but everything happened so fast, so much, the yelling, the smoke, the hoofs of horses, flashing of swords, the blood and screams," her voice tapered off to a whisper, "and he did look very powerful and attractive."

She looked up and noticed the dawn light now glowed faintly through her window and continued, "he repeated, louder this time, 'Why did you do this? We trusted you.'" Her body trembled, "then he pulled out his sword. I could hear the metal blade slide across his scabbard as it came out. I could smell the sweat from his horse, hear his armor rattle as he moved closer to me." Rebecca hesitated, "I don't want to talk anymore. It's like living it all over again." "Keep going, keep talking, my dear. You need to get it all out," Anna said soothing her daughter.

Rebecca sobbing, "Then, another soldier rode up to him and said, 'Celonius, the trap has worked, shall I order the second attack?' The Centurion turned back to me and said, 'Now you'll see the result of your treachery.' He nodded to the soldier, 'Yes, reform for the second attack.'" Rebecca's hands started to shake, she covered her face, "I didn't understand what all of that meant. Then he trotted close to me, reached out for me, clenched his fist and was grabbing me by my neck and said in a deep angry voice, 'But first, I'll deal with you myself, you treacherous whore…'

"I didn't know what he meant and why he was blaming me. I remember shaking my head and screaming, 'No! No! I didn't do anything. You don't understand, I came here to stop …' But before I could say anymore, I felt his strong hand tightened around my neck, his sword looming right in front of my face. I pushed free and fell off my horse. I tried to get up and run, I was terrified. But he was on top of me in an instant; he held me down, and held his sword to my neck. I could feel the blade almost piercing my skin.

"Then the spiraling started again and I flew up into a vortex. The screams and horrors still rang in my ears, this Celonius ready to kill me flooded my being, the smell of blood and huts aflame burned my nostrils, and then, I woke up here in my bedroom." Shaking and sobbing, Rebecca clutched her mother.

"No wonder you screamed, dear one, I would have also," Anna said as she put her arms around her daughter and hugged her tightly. "Now what does all this mean? When and where did you go? And why did you experience this now, right after you met the American archeologist?" Anna stood up to leave, "It is still early my dear, rest and let your mind settle, you will sleep deep and well now."

CHAPTER 22
Survey of the Site

We met back at the hill at 9 AM. Rebecca stood next to her red pickup truck as I pulled up. "Charles has headed back to the University with your mother's contract and sends his regards," I said. "Thank you, let's go," she said as we walked toward the trees that surrounded the ruins. The site proved as fascinating today as it did when we first walked this ancient ground.

"This is marvelous, simply marvelous," I said. The buildings in this site, about the size of a football field, lie in a north to south pattern. The church appears to be in the middle of the site. I could identify the main door by the column-like frame that still stood, but only to shoulder height. The top of the walls which were also no more than shoulder height and were jagged, their upper sections broken off ages ago, looked like the rugged peaks of a distant mountain range. They stood in silent testimony to the roof they supported and the people that stood within them nearly sixteen centuries ago and four centuries before that, the Roman soldiers who probably used this building as their command post.

The rest of the site, from what I could see through the shrubs and tree branches contained two other main structures and smaller buildings. We stood at the perimeter of the site, feeling the gentle breeze, a warming sign of spring, blue sky, a few puffy white clouds while the tree and shrub-studded archeological site lay before us.

I felt the elation of being at an ancient site ripe for a dig. These old ruins held a hidden story that begged to be told. I'm ready to find the beginning, the middle of the plot and the ending. But the trauma from the other night's time travel still haunted me. As I looked at the site, a wave of nausea rose up from my stomach, like fog rising from an early morning field. Was it here that Celonius executed Titus? I could hear and feel a whisper of a much more profound tale, a shrouded mystery whispered in my ear and sang its alluring seductive hymn deep in my mind. That's the story I really wanted to find. My nausea subsided. All of this passed through my mind in the few seconds that Rebecca and I stood at the edge of the site. "Ready to start," I said. "Oh, can I help?" she asked like a young schoolgirl. "Sure," I said. I smiled inwardly, 'Elliot, it doesn't get any better than this, ancient site, beautiful woman, beautiful day.'

"I don't have any archeological experience but just tell me what I can do," Rebecca said. "Well, let's see now. Hmmmm, no archeological experience, huh?" I said. 'Time to have some fun,' I thought. "OK, raise your right hand," I said with a half smile. Rebecca caught on, smiled and raised her right hand. "Do you, Rebecca Gilcrist, solemnly swear to perform the duties of an archeologist, so help you God?" I said. "Yes, I do," she responded, her smile broadened as she stood at attention. "Then, by the powers vested in me by the errrr, ahhh, The World Archeological Council, I hereby award you the title of A.I.T. - Archaeologist In Training. Do you accept your new title?" "Yes, I do," she said.

"Congratulations," I said and shook her hand, which felt, warm and vibrant, just wonderful to touch. Still smiling, "Great, now what do I do, where do we start?" she asked. I stepped a little closer to her, to enjoy the moment a little more, to feel closer to her, to somehow share with her the experience. I opened up my backpack and took out a laser distance-measuring device and placed it on the clipboard. Rebecca didn't step back but seemed to welcome my advance by firmly standing her ground. In fact, she seemed to lean forward toward me. I explained how the laser device worked and how we would measure the site and record the results. Being closer to her, along with her interest in the archeology of the site thrilled me. A surge of joy rose in me.

We spent the next three hours mapping the site. We started methodically at the center, with the church or command post and made general measurements and sketches of the structure. I used the laser finder to measure the distances of the other buildings to the church and a sextant device to measure angles. I would call out my findings to Rebecca who quite competently recorded the data into a near professional quality schematic of the site. We worked and developed a natural teamwork that I've rarely experienced before except when Charles and I worked a site together. By late afternoon, we had the entire site mapped out on my large 11 x 17 clipboard.

We sat down under a tree to examine our work with the clipboard in front of us so we could both look at it together. Years of experience taught me that one could really build up an appetite working outdoors for hours on end. I packed enough snacks and soft drinks for both of us.

"Tell me about what makes you such a diligent archeologist," Rebecca asked. Somewhat embarrassed, "Well, I think out of the box, if you will, while I follow standard archeological protocol, I also get insights from hunches and dreams." "Dreams? About what?" she asked. Getting even more embarrassed, I said, "let it suffice to say that I've dabbled a bit into what you may call 'reincarnation' and, well, although it may sound odd, this other worldly dream-like phenomenon has provided me with some rewarding insights."

I wanted to shift the conversation away from me, "But, Rebecca, tell me about you and your interest in this site. From what I've been told, you have a solid business background." She spoke of her college years and her interest in economics and business applications. Also, how some of her intuitive insights have led to new ventures for her company.

"But deep inside, I've always held a wonderment of metaphysics, the bridges between reality and the spiritual world are fascinating. I had an experience when I was just 18 that opened this world up to me." "Can you tell me about it? I'm interested," I said. Rebecca leaned forward, "I was driving mother to Glastonbury. Halfway there, I started to get a nervous feeling all over me. It was quite a strange sensation to say the least, as I had driven this route many times before and was quite familiar with the roads. When we got closer to town, the road curved sharply with some steep hills. As we approached a long section that curved up and to the left, an overwhelming urge came over me to stop and pull off to the side of the road. So I said, "Mother, I have to pull over to the side, I don't know why but I just have to."

I slowed, pulled over to the shoulder and slammed on the brakes. Simultaneously, I heard a loud horn and up the road, a lorry, or what you Yanks call a truck, came careening down the hill nearly out of control. It slid over into my lane, went screaming by with its horn blasting, brakes screeching. I know if I had not pulled over exactly when I did, it would have smashed right into us and at that speed it would have killed mother and me. Mother just stared at me, not with a sense of surprise but more with a sense of satisfaction. "Thank you for saving our lives Rebecca," mother said. "But more so thank you for listening to and following your intuitive impulse. That was quite a remarkable feat of intuitive guidance."

She paused for a moment then continued, "I've had other experiences like that, I get intuitions, feelings to do something or say something that always turned out to be the right thing to do or say. And, also, I have had an intense dream, perhaps of another life, quite terrifying. I really cannot talk about it right now."

I sensed a fear or insecurity come over her. I took her hand and held it gently but firmly. We sat in silence realizing for that moment, that in some way, we had a deep connection through our experiences. "Thanks for sharing that with me, Rebecca," I said in a near whisper. She nodded, and to break the spell held up the clipboard for me to look at. "What do you think about this unique layout, Elliot?"

CHAPTER 23
The Legend of the Stone

A general picture of the site became quite apparent to me: a central church or originally the Roman command post, another large building probably the dwelling for the monks or the Roman barracks, longer support buildings for animals, grain storage or workshops. "Quite ingenious the way the monks laid out the building plan. All structures aligned on a north/south axis, easy access to everything, one building's doorway leads to the next building's entrance, adequate spacing for worshipers to gather, and so why do we think that these were primitive people?" Rebecca asked as she intently looked over her work.

I rushed to swallow my oat nut granola bar so I could answer her. I raised my hand and pointed to my chomping mouth making some errant sounds, which was my way to signal her to wait for an answer. She smiled again. Finally, after gulping down some water to clear my throat. I replied "primitive technically maybe but otherwise just as smart as we are."

I leaned closer to the clipboard and just a bit closer to Rebecca at the same time, "If we had a typical layout of a first century CE Roman cavalry fort and superimposed it on your drawing, they'd match almost identically. Further proof that this Christian structure was built onto a previously built Roman structure."

"How can you tell if this was the church of St. Leo?" Rebecca asked. Surprised, I asked, "you know about St. Leo?" "Yes, there are many local legends I'm familiar with," she said. I replied, "his story fascinates me and I would love to see if this site connects to him. First, we'd have to find artifacts for carbon dating, some remains, inscriptions and the like. We'd compile the results and look for the smoking gun."

"What about the stone?" she asked. "The stone? What stone?", I asked. I raised my eyebrows and emphasized the questioning tone of my inquiry like a teacher asking an errant student to repeat an irrelevant comment.

"Yes, the stone, the legend of St. Leo's stone? Haven't you ever heard of it? St. Leo's stone?" Rebecca said with as much inquisitiveness as my question. But then she hesitated as if she said something she shouldn't have. "Can't say that I have. Sounds interesting, though. Tell me about it?" I asked. "Well it's only a legend, just a legend that grows and changes with the telling. You know, like the fountain of youth." She hesitated then continued, "well, it has been said that St. Leo had a magic stone which would bring peace to anyone who came near it. Looks like we need something like that today to send to all the world leaders," Rebecca laughed then said, "the legend says he also could cure people who had disease, injuries like broken limbs and the like." Somewhat skeptical I responded, "there are a few legends that turn out to be true but many don't. The 'stone' may be just one of those that just don't make the grade. Especially if it healed sick people, I mean that sounds like King Arthur's Excalibur sword stuck inside a magical stone." I then added, "and, I think we have enough work here that'll keep us busy for quite some time, let alone proving a tale about a magical stone." She raised her arms in frustration, "I don't know why I'm telling you about it, just thought you should know."

She became quiet and somewhat withdrawn and I could feel a growing tension. Somehow a sore nerve had been touched and I couldn't figure out why. As I thought this, I felt a sinking feeling in my stomach and a slight shortness of breath in my lungs. Was there more to this stone legend that I shouldn't brush it aside? Did she feel I was rejecting her, and not the legend of the stone? Rebecca looked down at her watch, "Oh, I must be getting back. We're just about finished here, right?"

"Yes, mission accomplished," I said as I stood up extending my hand to help lift her up. "No thank you, I can do it quite easily myself," she said. Rebecca turned and looked at me quite sharply. "You don't believe me do you?" she said. I sensed she interpreted my questions as a rejection of her revelation about the stone. Here she is trying to add information to our investigation and now she thinks I'm challenging her. At a loss for words, I fought a sense of confusion that started to loom over me. I realized the terror

I experienced in my second vision and that conflicted with the thrill of laying out the site with her. This placed me on an emotional roller coaster, which led me to a sort of bravado that rejected her stone legend. I then felt how absurd my initial protest to her story had been.

We didn't talk much on the way back to our vehicles. The momentum in our new relationship had been lost. "You know," she said, "for a guy who believes in dreams and reincarnation I'm wondering why the sacred stone of St. Leo seems so farfetched for you?" I lowered my head and in a soft voice confessed, "You're right, you're right and I'm sorry. I truly apologize for being skeptical about the sacred stone," Her eyes softened a bit. With a sense of satisfaction she said, "Well, finally, a man who listens and doesn't argue to prove he's right. Thank you Elliot for being 'in the moment.'" I responded, "why yes, and thank you for being honest and up front about this."

Quiet for a moment, she smiled then laughed. So did I. I grabbed her hand held it tight. She did the same. Like a teenage couple, we laughed and smiled at each other. "Some legends can be substantiated with evidence while others always remain just a legend. Sometimes they are legend and we are better off that way. Our psyche needs to believe in legends and myths. They keep our imaginations alive as well as giving us an internal drive to keep searching, keep striving," I said.

Admiration filled her eyes, "that's about the best explanation of legends I've ever heard. Thank you for saying that. It kind of takes the pressure off us as we always try to figure things out and get to the bottom of a story." I asked, "tell me more about the legend of the stone." "The legend is about a mystical stone, not sure how big it is, maybe a foot or so long. It's said to bring a sublime peace to anyone who comes close to it. Some say it'll affect you as far as 100 meters away although no one has ever found it or felt that sublime peace," she said.

"Where did you hear about this legend?" I asked. She replied, "I first heard about it when I went to grade school and one of my teachers told us. The whole class was enraptured; I still remember the feeling of awe and surprise when she told us. Of course, Mrs. Stevens being somewhat of an actress used her performance skills to add that extra drama to the story". "Do you believe the legend is true?" I asked. Rebecca's enthusiastic belief in the story made her eyes light up "…and yes! I believe it. It has to be true if it's lasted so long. St Leo lived 1600 years ago and his legend is still around. Not only talked about in the local school, but at the pubs and frat houses at the college. If you go to the library, you'll find a research paper on St Leo and the mythical stone. Besides, mystery surrounds the Glastonbury area and its legends of Jesus being there as a boy, Mary Magdalene and Joseph of Arimathea built the first Christian Church in 37 CE, Joseph planting his staff in the ground and it sprouting into a Thorn Tree, Mary Magdalene Street, the legend of the Fairy King living in the realms over the Tor, the Chalice Well, the legends go on and on."

I felt a bit uneasy to dispute her view on the legend but the early Christians had no interest in Celtic nature worship. By the fifth century, the Church was holding a tighter rein on their core teachings and frowned on anything remotely foreign to it.

She continued, "some say it's a sorcerer's stone left over from the Druids. Others say that the family of Jesus came here from Palestine and left their energy on the stone. What do you believe? I mean if the legend is true… which story is most feasible?" I didn't sense her question as a trap to draw me into believing the legend. I actually believe the story contrary to established Christian teachings that Jesus did have a wife, Mary Magdalene; recent discoveries of ancient scriptures have alluded to this. There is a legend that Jesus and Mary had a daughter, Sarah. It is possible, after the crucifixion, Mary and Sarah may have traveled to England. "If the legend is true, I think the Druids and the family of Jesus joined together to infuse their beliefs into the stone."

"You mean both of them blessed the stone?" Rebecca asked. I replied, "Yes, think about it, it makes sense. If Jesus really taught what is in the Gnostic Gospels, his family would be open to certain Druid teachings. It makes sense that if indeed Mary Magdalene came here she would have been welcomed probably by a Druid priestess." She smiled, "I never looked at it that way, makes sense. How do the Romans fit into this?" "They provided the impetus for the family to move. I'm sure the Jewish authorities in Palestine viewed the followers of Jesus and their teachings as a big threat to the establishment. The Pharisees and priests probably prodded the Romans to exterminate them in order to keep peace in that part of the Empire. The Romans figured the Jewish leaders held more control over the people than this upstart cult, so they probably enforced whatever was asked of them."

"So you think that's why the holy family moved to Britannia? But didn't the Romans invade Britannia also?" she asked. "Yes, but slowly at first. It took them decades to spread west and north. But undoubtedly, the holy family was caught up in the turmoil of native Celts battling the Romans. The Romans also hunted down the Druids because they fiercely protected their mysteries, conducted, according to the Romans, brutal human sacrifices and conspired with the general population against Roman rule. The holy family, who were peace-loving, probably held a neutral position, but it may have been difficult for them not to take sides."

"So what do you think the holy family did?" Rebecca asked. "They either moved further north to Scotland or to southern France where local legends tell of them," I replied. "I'm sure they left their mark here in Britain even if they were only here for a few decades," Rebecca said. "Oh, I'm sure they did as you mention before about the Christian legends of Glastonbury. But its getting late," I said. "Can we continue our conversation, tonight, say at dinner?" I asked

Rebecca paused for a moment; her eyes glistened, "Why yes. There's a wonderful pub in town called, 'The Kings Bridge' I'll pick you up at your hotel at 7."

CHAPTER 24
Sharing Dreams at the Pub

I spent the rest of the day compiling the data we collected and comparing it to other known ruins. I would stop occasionally to anticipate my meeting with Rebecca. I needed to tell her about my other reality experiences so she could understand the mystery and significance of the site.

I thought we had arrived at the point of knowing each other well enough to talk about our dream experiences. I felt mine was especially weird with my execution of Titus, the planned massacre of the village and the betrayal of this woman that led to the Romans being caught off guard. If I told her in a simple quiet voice without any emotion or fanfare, she might accept it more or less as 'matter of fact.' Plus, I'm going to hear about her dream; who knows, sharing dreams may give us more in common.

Right on time, Rebecca pulled up to my hotel in her sports car and stepped out. Dressed in a flowing dress with a coordinated scarf, earrings and necklace, Rebecca looked absolutely stunning as well as elegant. She walked straight to me, hugged me and kissed me quickly and gently on both cheeks. Somehow words fumbled out of my mouth, "Wow! You look beautiful." "Kind of handsome yourself, cowboy," she replied as she grabbed my hand and led me to her convertible. We drove to the center of town and parked as short walk to the pub.

Celtic artwork and artifacts, along with adornments of England's royalty decorated the walls of 'The Kings Bridge'. I could see the appropriateness of the pub's name, its facade bridging the monarchy to the natural mystery worlds of the Isles. We sat down in a corner table, ordered and sat back to enjoy each other's company. "How appropriate that we have supper here," I said. "Yes, that's why I chose it and I think its time that we spoke about our dreams," Rebecca said, "I think that will somehow give us an insight as to why we're so into this adventure." "Personally, I thought it was my good looks and charming personality," I said with a smile. "Yes, but don't forget to mention your humble and quiet demeanor," she teased back.

"Ok, you got me," I replied, "Let me tell you about my dream first." I reviewed my first dream, the brief time I took on the persona of a Roman Centurion, swimming in the river, which eventually led to my first major discovery, the Roman fort that catapulted me into fame as well as secured my position as an early Britannia archeologist. Rebecca paid close attention, asking a few questions. At the closing of this dream story, she said, "My God Elliot, how revealing, how real, especially when Dr. Duningham confirmed that what you heard in Latin actually translated into a meaningful part of the story. Go on please, I'm interested in your second dream."

In minute detail, I told her my second more intense dream, the smells and sensations of the horse stables, the soldiers, the report of the legion being surrounded, the execution of the pacifist soldiers, and the attack on the village. Her reaction turned from interest, to shock and horror. "Oh, Elliot, my God, it was you, you rode up to me, you blamed me, you killed them all, the screams, the cries, it was you who led the soldiers, the Romans on black horses with silver armor." Her eyes welled up with tears; she stood up and ran for the door. Dumbfounded, I got up and ran after her.

As I passed by a table where an older couple sat, the gentlemen said, "Really old chap, you've got to do better than that." I caught up to her in front of the pub where she stopped, hiding her face in her hands. "What is it Rebecca? Did I say something to offend you? I'm sorry if I did..." "No, no," she responded, "your dream experience.... my dream, they're almost the same. Except, the village, the massacre you planned, was in my dream, and I don't think it's a dream anymore nor a vision, it was so real, and I was there. The screaming, the cries, the fire, the choking smoke, the dead animals, babies, the desperation." She started to shake, her body went limp, and she began to collapse. I grabbed her, embraced her, and held her closely to me. I have never shared such an intimate moment as this in all my life. I walked her gently to a bench in a small park next to the pub. "Sit down, dear, you need not say any more, I know, I understand," trying to comfort her.

"No you don't understand, Elliot. You lived in your dreams or whatever they are. But I didn't, I was attacked, thrown to the ground and you stood over me with your sword at my neck, did you execute me too during the massacre?" she stopped and started to sob. I just held her tightly, slowly rocking her. "Ok, you can stop now... say no more, it'll just take you deeper into it." She pushed me back, "I need to go deeper into it, I need to tell you one last thing, Elliot, the final thing that happened before everything went dark," she paused, took a deep breath and in an instant, took control of herself.

Rebecca pointed at me, "It was you!" "What? Me... what do you mean?" I recoiled. "It was you who tried to kill me. Or, did you really kill me?" she said while poking me in the chest. I starred at her with both concern and disbelief, ready to counter her statement with a protest of innocence. I paused to compose my answer but in a flash, it came to me that maybe I did, maybe I did kill her. I already knew I executed Roman soldiers who refused to fight. I said to her, "Wait, go back and tell me the whole story of what happened. Talk slowly if you can." Rebecca told of the Roman cavalry on black horses with shinning Roman armor riding through a village of screaming running women and children. With their dwellings ablaze and smoke everywhere, the Romans systematically butchered the village animals, the elders, the women and children. "Then in the horror of it all, I sat on my horse trying to stop this massacre, gasping for air when a Roman officer who I knew, a Centurion, named Celonius, rode up to me, called me a traitor and a harlot, screaming this was all my fault, he grabbed for me and I fell off of my horse. In an instant he was on top of me, he pulled out his sword and pointed into my neck and screamed, 'Why? I loved you, why did you do this to us? You betrayed me, all of us, now die!'"

She sobbed and shook violently and jumped up. "You bastard, murderer, how could you," she screamed while pointing at me. "Rebecca, Rebecca, snap out of it, you're here, now, in this century, this time," I implored as I stood up to hold her. She pushed me back, screamed, "you son of a bitch." In one swift motion, she raised her hand and slapped me then turned and ran toward her car. I started after her when I was pulled back.

"Hold it bloke. Leave her alone!" a deep male voice said as my body spun around, forced to turn by his strong hands. I came face to face with the town constable. He shoved me against the brick wall of the building behind us, spun me around and snapped handcuffs on me. "Heard you were causing Ms. Rebecca quite a problem. I heard her crying, called you a murderer she did. These folks called about you chasing her out of the pub," he pointed to the older couple who were now standing outside the pub. They looked at me with a stern unforgiving look.

I stood dumbfounded, but before I could say a word in my defense, Rebecca came rushing back from her car. "Oh, Constable Grayson, no need, this is my friend Elliot from

America. We were practicing our lines for a play and he's real good at it. I had to run away crying, its just part of the script," Rebecca announced now with tears dried and a smile on her face. She turned to the older couple, "No problem here, he's a good friend and fellow drama student. Look, see," and with that Rebecca cupped my face in her hands and kissed me softly and slowly on my lips.

"Well, ok now," said the constable while he un-cuffed me, "it has been a long night, time for you 'drama students' to get along." The older couple turned their frowns into smiles and nodded. And I, just stood there, not saying a word relishing the feeling of Rebecca's lips on mine. She took my hand and walked me back to the car.

We drove in silence, through the town and onto the road that led to her home. "We have a small cottage on the estate. Its empty now, not in use, we can go there and talk about what happened," she said as she turned onto the drive of the estate. "You mean by 'what happened' the constable and the kiss you gave me or your reaction to my dream story?" I asked. She reached over and squeezed my hand, "We'll talk about the kiss later on. I need to tell you my complete dream so you can see how both of our stories are linked together."

Although much shorter than my journey back to the cavalry fort, the attack on the legion, the rebellion and execution and Celonius' plan to attack the village as a diversion to rescue the legion, Rebecca's story dovetailed into mine. But more importantly, the blending of our stories showed us that we were also together nearly 2000 years ago. "It sounds like we were," I hesitated to say lovers even though I saw Celonius and Venetia passionately kissing in my second vision. "I mean we must have known each other quite well back then." "I think that's putting it mildly. We more than knew each other, somehow we were involved," she replied. "Do you have feelings at all from your experience? You were raging mad when you knocked me off my horse accusing me of treachery," she asked.

"I knew that when I first saw you Rebecca," the words gushed out of me like water from a deep underground well. "I felt as if I've known you before even though we just met. Not only did I have that feeling but much more. You're so nice to look at and so nice to be with, Rebecca. How can I feel anger?" However, I would soon find out, my anger lurked waiting for the right moment to jump out.

She touched my hand and squeezed it gently. "I know Elliot, I know, but much of this comes from back then. We're different people now. That's all I want to say. I just can't talk more about 'us' right now. Let's first find out what happened back then." She hesitated for a moment, looked at me, "But just to make sure," she stopped the car, wrapped her arms around my neck and kissed me again with her soft moist lips. I held her tightly, drew her closer to me. "Not yet Elliot," she said and gently but firmly pulled back from me, rev'd the engine and sped down the road. "We need to discover more about the situation back then. Elliot, do you have any ideas on how we can do that?"

An image of Charles flashed before me. 'Yes, he's back, he can help us,' I thought, 'his logical insightful mind can get to the bottom of this.' "Charles," I said, "let's go see Charles at the hotel". Breaks squealed, my seat belt press into my chest as Rebecca turned the car around and raced toward the hotel.

CHAPTER 25
Back to the Cave

We found Charles on the back sitting porch of the hotel clustered in the corner away from the few other guests spread out along the porch and adjoining gardens. He seemed silently delighted that we barged in on him as he relaxed after his drive back from the University. Puffing on his trusted pipe, the air filled with the aromatic smoke of his tobacco. "I remember the time when you could smoke all you wanted in the privacy of your hotel room. Now with all these confounded smoking laws, we have to go outside to experience the pleasures of simply smoking a pipe can surely bring you," Charles said slowly swaying in an antique rocking chair. "Was your survey of the site successful?"

I briefly updated him on our survey results. "But Charles, Rebecca had a dream vision back in time that you must listen to," I said. Rebecca then told him of her dream vision of the massacre of the village. In the stunned silence that followed I said, "Charles as we see it, Rebecca's dream picks up where my story ends. She's in the village being attacked by Roman cavalry, the attack that I had planned as a diversion to relieve the legion encircled by the Celts," I looked over to Rebecca who nodded in agreement. He looked at us, puffed some more, "You've considered of course that this could be a coincidence or that maybe you both saw the same movie when you were children and its now popping back in your memories?"

"You don't really believe that do you?" I asked. "Of course not, but you know that's what a lot of other people will think. No, Elliot and Rebecca, I believe your stories implicitly. We did find the ruins of a Roman fort and advanced Britain's archeological record substantially based on one of your dreams, Elliot. Yes, I do believe you both." "Then what do we do about it Dr. Weldon?" Rebecca asked.

"Rebecca dear, please call me Charles. It seems to me," Charles paused to puff up a cloud of smoke, "that all of these dreams, related dreams, I must add, are messages to you both. Messages from the past about this massacre, the destruction of the village, but also a personal message to both of you."

"I can get an idea what the message is about," I said. "Apparently, I ordered the destruction of the village and also knew Rebecca back then. Not only did I have the village destroyed but," I lowered my head and spoke slowly "but I personally attacked Rebecca." I lowered my head into my hands, close to weeping at the thought of harming this sweet lovely woman. She slid her chair next to mine, reached over and hugged me, ran her fingers through my hair and softly rubbed her hand down my back.

"Elliot, Elliot, dear Elliot, look at what you've done. You brought all of this to the surface so we can heal it. We can make it right now after all these centuries. You've helped us answer so many questions in our lives." Her voice and her touch comforted me. I could feel some ancient energy rise up within me, the power of Celonius, that ancient warrior I used to be, seemed now to be in my head as I was in his during my dreams. I looked at Charles while I took Rebecca's hand, kissed it and held it by my side. Rebecca asked, "Charles, do you have any suggestions on what we're supposed to do if anything? Why is this happening to us now? To me?"

Charles put down his pipe, "If there's one thing that my life-long devotion to archeology has taught me," he leaned forward, "the earth, the ground, holds a resonance, a vibration or frequency, of all events that take place on it and the more powerful the event, the stronger the resonance. I could feel it while walking on an ancient battlefield, now covered with acres of farmland, grazing cows and fields of wheat. I knew something happened there. We cannot measure these vibrations or memories with any instruments because," and he looked directly at me, "as Doctor Duningham told you, they exist on another plane of reality, if you will, a place our science is starting to explore but doesn't yet realize what it is all about. However, the human soul, the human spirit, does and can experience these other dimensional resonances. And remember, my dear explorers, much of modern medical science says that we do not have a spirit, we do not have an etheric energy that belongs to us," he paused for a second to let the impact of his words sink in.

"It's the other way around. We belong to Spirit, to God if you will, and for the most part Spirit presents key events in our lives for us to experience and or work out.

"So it's not by happenstance that this happened to both of you, particularly at almost the same time," Charles picked up his pipe and began puffing clouds of smoke. Rebecca lifted her hands in a gesture of protest and confusion, "But I've lived here for all of my childhood and came back often over the past years. I've never experienced any dreams or visions so vividly real as this one. Why now?" "Who knows for sure why these events happen. We are all actors in a play written by God, but I will guess that the reason is sitting right next to you," Charles said pointing to me.

"Me? Explain please." "Both of you think about it," Charles put down his pipe and leaned forward. "Rebecca, have you had dreams like this before or have you had any psychic like experiences?" "No dreams or visions that even came close to this one, its realness made me feel as though I was actually there. I did have many intuitions, however, some quite dramatic, but powerful reality type dreams, no," she replied.

"So along comes this American or former Roman Centurion, if I may," Charles politely nodded toward me, "and, by Jove, you have a full blown Roman Celtic reality experience. Further, I will dare to say, walking on this ancient hidden site also fired up this experience because, I venture, this site could well be where the two of you met or lived two millennia ago." "But why is this happening, Professor?"

Rebecca grabbed Charles' hands, "you've explained 'how' it happened but what is the reason behind it?" I sat there more or less like a spectator unable to speak. The enormity and depth of what was being said and what we had experienced overwhelmed me. Charles stood up and walked to the edge of the porch, which by now had been vacated by the other guests who had finished their cigarettes. "I wish I knew, perhaps, to clear some old debts, emotional debts which the Hindu's call karma. Don't forget, somehow, hundreds if not thousands of people were massacred because of you two."

"But what did I do to be part of that? Elliot's role seems rather clear, leading the attack as a military diversion," Rebecca looked at me with genuine understanding. "Rebecca, somehow you were involved because of my berating you as a traitor. Don't you think?" I said opening my hands to emphasize my question. "Let's all be quiet and 'not think' about this because all of this does defy logical thinking," Charles said. "Sit still and relax all tension from your body. Call it meditation if you will but let's see if anything comes to us." We all took a deep breath and quieted ourselves. The silence of the night soon took over. An engine from a motorcycle far away droned into silence as its rider rode deeper into the night.

I found it difficult at first to quiet my mind as extraneous thoughts drifted in and out. I opened my eyes just a bit and glanced over at Rebecca who had propped herself up and sat elegantly in the yoga meditation position. Charles sat quietly, eyes closed, with a child-like look on his face. Feeling a bit guilty that my companions seemed to take to silent meditation like a fish to water, I took a deep breath and tried to relax. Having remembered a technique in a stress relief workshop I attended during my undergrad days, I placed my left hand over my heart and took slow deep breaths. On the third deep breath, I exhaled and coughed, a good sign as coughing is said to be a sign of clearing stress from your body.

I felt calm and relaxed; my breathing became slower, soothing, and rhythmic. And then it happened, the spinning, like I'm on a ride slowly rotating clockwise, what Dr. Duningham called entering the Traversable Wormhole. Then comes the sound like a heavy rain shower. Even though I have encountered this spinning and noise before, I'm still shaken and afraid although not as badly. The spinning increased but instead of panic, a peace and tranquility flowed into me.

"Follow us Centurion, we are not far," a sweet and gentle woman's voice resonates. Her voice comes from in front of me. A second voice, male but soft and somewhat melodious comes from besides me, "Yes, almost there, watch your step." I'm now aware of the full weight of my body, the sensation of walking, my muscles, I feel the girth, my strength, and power in my stride. I am familiar with this feeling; I have felt it before swimming in the river and giving commands at the cavalry outpost. I am again Celonius, the Roman warrior. Vision comes to my eyes and I see a moon-lit path, a hillside and the figure of a robed woman ahead of me. She moves with elegance and grace, almost floating as we move toward the hillside in front of me.

I'm now fully conscious of being an observer looking out from behind the mind of this Roman, reading his thoughts. To my side is a young man, a teenager. He looks at me with a calm face yet I sense a touch of resentment in his eyes. The narrow pathway, covered with brush and along the slope of a hill, takes over my attention. 'Yes, watch my step indeed but I'm also watching for the sign of an ambush, 'Celonius thought. I could sense his alertness and his warrior instincts and as before, I felt our minds merging and, again, his thoughts are my thoughts.

My hand went down to my sword and I walked along with my hand on its hilt. Just in case. But the 'just in case' never came. The woman turned around and looked at me. Her deep green eyes radiated softly. I sensed the depth of the universe in her gaze. If the eyes are the windows to the soul, I have never seen a more beautiful soul… until last week. Me, Elliot merging with the ancient me gazing into the eyes of this ancient woman, saw Rebecca.

With her dazzling eyes, light skin, enthralling face and features, long flowing black hair, she put her hand on my hand that gripped the hilt. "Warrior of Rome, Centurion of the emperor, fear not an ambush. You are welcome here, again, be at peace. I am about to show you a sacred place that will change you forever." The words flowed out of her mouth like clear water springing from an exquisitely sculptured fountain.

Almost impulsively, my words flowed back, "Thank you for your honoring words, your grace and beauty bring me much pleasure but I am fine the way I am. I don't want to be changed for life." Pride welled up inside of me for who I am and what I had accomplished for the Empire. "Centurion, may I ask your name? Mine is Venetia, priestess of this loving land," she said her name and the intensity in her eyes drew me into a deeper connection with her. For a moment I felt like a young schoolboy on his first date, but the warrior in me took some control, "I am Celonius, Centurion and commander of the cavalry cohort of General Vespasian's Legion II Augusta."

"Very pleased to meet you Celonius. Although you wear armor for the Emperor, I can see you have a pure heart and there is no deceit within you. Tell me Celonius, do you feel anything in your heart, a feeling of peace and well being?" I didn't have to think about a response, immediately the words came out of me, "Yes, I do. I have sensed it right after we arrived in your land and started to build our fort on top of this hill. I felt it strongly tonight, I could not sleep; the gods are calling to me so I've gone out and walked to be alone so they could talk to me." I lowered my head, I guess as a sign of yielding to her, to the moment but more importantly, to my own heart. Soldiering meant nothing now, my psychological armor stripped off; I stood in revelation, and an awareness of someone within me I had never known before.

The state of oneness between Celonius and I, Elliot, split apart. I, Elliot, became detached to the me of the past and sat fully conscious of my archeologist self. I knew it was my turn to speak to Celonius, "Go with her, trust her, and find out what she is going to reveal to you." I wanted to know this ancient treasure she spoke of so in my present day I could go and find it, I would know where to look and maybe, just maybe, this could lead to the answer Rebecca, Charles and I were looking for.

Celonius took Venetia's hand and kissed it. I could feel the softness well up in his heart. He longed for the touch of a woman. The years of fighting, seeing valued friends die, some in his arms. I saw scenes of him as he held dying comrades and saw their life spill out of them as their blood anointed the ground where they died. All of these visions and feelings flashed before me and I knew in that moment, the pain and agony this man, this other me, had suffered in his life. Venetia's soft touch, the gentleness of her voice, the elegance of her body and the deep mystery glowing in her eyes, flowed over his and now my soul like a gentle rain over a dry hot parched desert. As these emotions shot through us, I felt guilty that I had pushed him to go with her but time has been bridged and the questions of the present may have answers from two millennia ago.

"Take me gentle woman, priestess of the gods of this land, I yield to you," he said lowering his head. She took off her scarf and wrapped it around his head forming a blindfold. Her scent engulfed us. Call them pheromones, but the effect seduced us into a contented fulfillment, a sensation that brought tears to this tired combat weary warrior.

We walked and for a while, I tried to keep track of how far we had traveled so when I became Elliot again in the 21st century, I would have an idea where to find this 'sacred place,' but, the human body being what it is, vertigo slowly crept into my senses. I could no longer tell if we turned left or right, walked up or down the trail, I gave up my effort of counting steps and turns. What I could tell, however, that a gentle sensation of well-being and peace gently relaxed and comforted me. "Do you feel that Celonius?" Venetia's soothing voice added to the placidity, "Do you feel the wonder of the mystery that came from the Joining?"

"I feel peace, so very much needed peace," Celonius spoke as if exhausted.

'Ask her where we are,' I whispered to Celonius and robotically he asked her, "Where are we?" I felt her scarf unravel from my head. I immediately sensed a pale light before my eyes gradually came into focus. We were in a cave as spacious as a room. In the center, lay a large stone that seemed to glow. Venetia's lips formed a gradual smile; her eyes glowed, in a soft tender voice she whispered, "Welcome." "Be seated," a boy-like voice coming from behind me, as firm hands guided me down to a stone like seat carved into the cave's wall. Celonius looked at Venetia's brother helping him sit down and I knew instantly who he was in the 21st century. I beheld the young face of Robin. He pointed to the stone, "Behold the Stone of the Joining. The source of the peace that grows inside of you."

"It is not necessary to fight anymore," Venetia said. "Let the magic of the stone guide you." Like an excited schoolboy who knew the answer to a difficult question, I whispered, "Ask her why it's called the Stone of the Joining?" Obediently, my

Roman counterpart asked her. Venetia's demeanor changed from gracious to serious, looking intently at Celonius, "15 years ago, a holy woman and her daughter came to our land from the lands beyond the great sea…" I jumped with enthusiasm inside Celonius's mind, 'the great sea is the Mediterranean, the lands beyond that would be Palestine…' but before I could say anymore, the spinning started; I knew I was heading back to my current time. 'No, not now, let me stay, I need to hear what she's going to say, this could change history, this could….'

CHAPTER 26
Anger and Rage Returns

I heard Charles whisper, "Elliot, what can change history? Come on old chap, hold onto it, hold on to that vision…" I awoke to see Charles starring at me intently with his finger over his lips and nodding toward Rebecca. I looked over to her, she sat there in a peaceful slumber and yes, I could not deny it. I saw it plainly, I saw Venetia in all of her grace, elegance and beauty sitting there. A wave of instant respect and bonding came over me. Somehow, I knew this woman two millennia ago and now, here we are, together again.

Then, like a dark shadow in the night, my admiration turned to malevolence and anger, I despised her, but why I did not know. The feelings of affection snuffed out by rage that seemed to be injected into my veins and flow throughout my body. Charles looked at me in astonishment, "Elliot, what's wrong? My God, you just changed from Dr. Jekyll into Mr. Hyde." "I don't know," I stood up and pointed at Rebecca, "but its her, she used me, she betrayed me, she's a harlot." I couldn't control it, the words just blurted out of me, beads of sweat bubbled on my forehead, I felt nauseous, and my hands shook uncontrollably. Finally, my turn had come to have two thousand year old emotions jump into my present life.

Charles shot to his feet and stood between Rebecca and me. "Good grief more unbridled emotions from the ancient past. Nothing surprises me anymore. Go walk it off Elliot," Charles pointed to the pathway into the hotel garden, "Go vent over there, then come back and we'll work this out." His physical demeanor stiffened with a solid rock-like stance, blocking me. His powerful response so unlike his normal easy going lightness shocked me somewhat back to my normal self. I turned and stormed down the pathway not turning to look at Rebecca. My rage toward her still boiled. I didn't want to look at Rebecca; I became disgusted at even knowing her. If I did look at her, I would have seen her tears and the remorse that suffused her feminine countenance.

There is a certain type of trauma one suffers from a dramatic change of deep feelings. When I awoke from my dream vision in the cave, I felt the peace and serenity as I did in my journey back in time. The onset of anger and betrayal toward Rebecca seemingly out of the clear blue sky left me shaking and irrational. As I walked down the path, I wrestled with my anger. Why this sudden burst of animosity toward her? Why this intense shift of feelings? Surely I had no present day reason to feel this way, so the answer had to be the pain of having been betrayed by the beautiful woman I knew through Celonius in my second dream vision. As I once stood within Celonius' mind, now it seems, he stood within my mind with the rage of two thousand years erupting like a long dormant volcano.

I sat on a bench by the rose garden and took deep slow breaths. I visualized the air coming into my lungs as water quenching the fire that burned inside of me. Within 5 breaths, I began to settle down; a few more breaths and I could again think somewhat rationally.

I could now see the link between my three visions and could also see that I didn't receive them in the order that they actually occurred. The last vision in the cave of peace should have preceded the second vision of the rebellion. I realize now why I seemed so relaxed in my second vision then shocked when I heard the legion had been trapped. Also, I could see why some of my troops didn't want to fight. The Stone of the Joining had left its mark on them as well as me. And then there was Rebecca's vision with me calling her a traitor and taking out my anger on her by throwing her to the ground confirmed the order of the visions.

I returned to Charles and Rebecca eager to give them my insight on these visions as well as the story of the Stone of the Joining. As I came up to them, I could see Rebecca talking to Charles. She looked at me and an instant jolt of terror came over her. She grabbed onto Charles desperately pushing him between the two of us. At the same time, I could feel the anger start to rise again in me. But I had to fight it; this anger came from something that happened two thousand years ago not now. I stood on the path before them and started my deep breathing again. I thought of the Stone of the Joining and, surprisingly, I became calm and felt the anger subside and then disappear altogether.

"Elliot, Elliot, my colleague, have you settled down?" Charles asked. Smiling at Rebecca and Charles, "yes, I'm fine now," I responded. "Good come over here, and listen to Rebecca's vision," Charles looked at Rebecca, "are you alright my dear? Can you do this?" Rebecca took a deep breath and tried to compose herself. "I can't, I just can't, this is all too much for me. And what about him?" she asked pointing at me, her hand shook uncontrollably, her voice waivered, "will he try to kill me again?" "I know what this is about Rebecca," I said. A vision of Venetia showing me the Stone of the Joining flashed through my head. With a tone of understanding mixed with authority, I said, "Venetia, remember the Stone of the Joining, remember the Stone of the Joining."

"What?" Charles surprised at this unusual bit of new information. But not Rebecca, she closed her eyes and within seconds she became calm. In another few seconds, she became radiant returning once again to her unique form of femininity. Her eyes closed, she smiled and slowly nodded, "Yes, oh my dear God, yes, I remember, I see it, I can still feel it."

"Will someone please tell me what's going on?" Charles said, surprise and confusion rippling through his face. "Elliot," Rebecca said. She stood up, her fear gently swept away and replaced with affection, stepped toward me. "Yes, the Stone, the Stone." We opened our arms and embraced. I did not anticipate the feeling of warmth and compassion I felt for her. All feelings of anger had slipped away, replaced by this new sensation of tenderness. By the way she embraced me, I knew Rebecca felt the same way. I tuned out our surroundings, Charles, the hotel, the garden, and just reveled in the sweetness of being close to Rebecca and Venetia. The thought of both them, although the same woman, but in different physical bodies separated by two millennia, knowing Celonius, the brave leader and myself, somewhat a scholar, gave me comfort as well as a thrill. As we embraced, time seemed endless, broken abruptly by Charles.

"Ok, what stone? What joining? Need I remind you two love birds that we're on a scientific archeological fact finding mission."

CHAPTER 27
Rebecca's Vision in the Garden

We slowly moved apart and looked at Charles, smiling at our revelation. He opened his hand and gestured us to our seats. "Well thank you all for returning to the present. Elliot, I need you to tell us your story while it's fresh in your mind. Was this Stone of the Joining a part of it? I think this stone, from an archeological standpoint, has great significance. So go ahead and don't mind if I take notes." Charles said.

I told my dream vision in the minutest detail. Both Charles and Rebecca asked questions but not so many as to break the flow of my story. "I was Venetia," Rebecca said. "I think I know now why you tried to kill me and accused me of betrayal." "Yes," said Charles, "I can see the link." "I think I can too, but I'm still a bit fuzzy about it," I said. "You need to hear Rebecca's story that she told me when you walked through the garden. It will clarify it all," Charles said. Rebecca looked at me with soft yet piercing eyes. "When I closed my eyes and became silent, I almost immediately went into a spinning sensation. Then I heard voices; men's voices, they were talking to me. They called me Venetia."

"Oh, this is getting better and better," I said, "but keep going."

"I awoke, if that's the right word, in a dimly lit room. Three men sat across from me. My dress and robe were that of a priestess or lady of magic adorned with crystals and colored stones, which I assumed to be emeralds. While I looked stately, our conversation resembled gutter talk," Rebecca leaned back in her chair and composed herself.

"I recognized the two closest to me. They were my brothers Bret, the other, Finian, much younger, barely a teenager. Both were bare chested, wore leggings bound with leather straps, a leather like waistband and brass arm rings. Bret wore a cape, Finian did not. Both very handsome, I felt love for them, especially Finian, but distress lingered deep within me. What they asked of me fueled my anxiety." Rebecca took a deep breath and leaned forward, "the third man, somewhat dark and sinister looking, sat behind them. I recognized his dress as Druid but from a different area far from our village. I sensed his energy as vile but quite powerful."

Bret coaxed me, "Sister, sleep with this Roman Centurion, seduce him, lay with him, become his lover, talk with him and listen for information that could help our cause." "And what cause is that?" I asked. "To rid our sacred land of these Roman invaders. They defile the earth, they kill our people if we don't cooperate with them, they take our gold, sleep with our women, enslave our children to work on their bridges and buildings," Bret said as he clenched his fists tightly. "We are slowly losing our ways, our cultural identity," Finian added. The Druid smiled and nodded. I could see now the influence he had on my brothers.

"So you want me to sleep with him, become his lover, and get information about the Romans?" I asked more out of curiosity although rage began bubbling up within me. "Exactly, this information will help our cause as I said before. Surely, sister as a priestess you would want us to win out over these invaders," Bret said nodding his head in reassurance. "And what of our sacred land and honor, would our ancestors condone this trickery?" My anger started to reveal itself. "Sister, for our people, you and your body will be our weapon that destroys our enemy," Finian said adding emphasis by pointing to my body. Shock ran through me at Finian's remark. Somehow, the traits of boyhood had left him, the yearning to be a man had snuffed out his innocence. "First dear brothers, let me tell you I am a priestess of our cosmic goddess, Brigantia, the bringer of spirit, light and power. Our mother, our grandmothers, as well as the other priestesses and their mothers going back for generations have trained me. I am also the Keeper of the Stone of the Joining, the stone that is infused with the Father wisdom of the Magdalene of the East and of the Mother Spirit of our land. Do you understand this?" I asked.

They both nodded somewhat impatiently. However, the Druid's body tensed; he leaned forward and sneered as I spoke of the Stone of the Joining. Despite their negativity, I continued, "And now, realizing that I represent the lineage of our ancestors as a priestess of light, you want me to be a harlot, sleep with a Roman, have sex with him, lie about my intentions and seduce him into telling me military secrets about his army," I said. "Yes, he is strong, handsome and dedicated to his cause; I am attracted to him and will lay with him if I so desire. But, there are secrets in our land, the Sacred Stone of the Joining and relics that carry the power of spirit that I will betray if I carry out your demands. I am distressed at your asking me to do this, you my brothers, who came from the same womb I did," I hung my head down, paused, then with a polite but fierce look, I said, "No! I will not do this. If we are to deal with the Romans it will be for peace, showing them the beauty of our land and people, not its treachery." Bret snapped back, "Sister, listen to us, you can be close to him and learn their plans, the information we need to know, their weaknesses, places they will march to, places where we can destroy them, places..." I raised my hand for him to stop.

Tears flowed from my eyes, their dishonor of me, their sister and priestess of the land, sent a sharp pain into my heart. "Stop! Enough! Enough! I will hear no more of this. I am not a spy or a harlot, I am a priestess.... and," my voice struggled to come out, "the Stone, have you ignored its message... it carries the future of our land... how could you both not feel it?'

After some silence, Bret said, "Yes, the Stone, that loving Stone, where was it when the Roman Cavalry rode through our village and we threw flowers instead of stones at them. It didn't stop them from taking over our land and village."

"Oh my brother, can't you see," I implored again, "they didn't ravage us, attack us, or rob us, they came and left in peace. Did you forget that? The peace energy of the Stone did that for us." Oblivious to my speaking of the Stone, Finian interrupted, "You are a member of our clan and come from a long line of clan leaders, if you won't help us, then you are a traitor and we will go on without you."

I looked directly at the Druid and fired back in anger, "and what is your business here? You are not from our land." He starred stone face at me. I outstretched my hands, "All of you, I implore you to reason this out. The Romans did not conquer all the known lands of the earth because they are fools. They are the supreme artisans of war and destruction, best to learn and understand them; when the winds howl and the rains fall in torrents, do you stand outside and swing your sword at the sky?"

"They seemed startled, perhaps the logic of my response made them think how risky their plan was. Finian tried to speak, another look of anger contorting his face. But before he could, Bret grabbed his arm, I could see his hand tightening, signaling his younger brother to be quiet, "You are right my sister, excuse us in our rashness, we are sorry for offending you and…" Then a counter clockwise spinning started along with a strange sound like heavy rainfall; I woke up back here in the garden."

Rebecca looked up. Glanced at Charles but locked her eyes on me. "I didn't betray you Elliot, I would never do that." I sat in silence, dumbfounded, overwhelmed with the unfolding stories of two thousand years ago being told now, today, about me, about Rebecca.

CHAPTER 28
Charles Puts it All together

Charles interrupted my thoughts, "Ok, this is how I see it, but first, yes, Elliot as you said before, these visions for some reason came to you out of the order of how they occurred in history. There may be a good reason for that which we're not aware of now. However, I see the story actually occurring like this:

"Elliot's first dream, Celonius, the Roman cavalry commander, in the process of building a fort by a river, receives orders to march westward.

"Elliot's third dream, Celonius, is walking with Venetia, a priestess, and her brother on a night path, on a hillside. She asks him to trust her; he, tired of war, agrees. He's taken to what appears to be a cave and has a spiritual experience possibly from a sacred artifact, a stone. He feels a profound peace. And, oh by the way, I hope you somehow can figure out where this cave is Elliot, it sounds like another archeological treasure trove. But I digress.

"Then comes Rebecca's second dream, her brothers are dressed in warrior's garb influenced by a strange Druid priest who is adversarial to peace and the influence of the 'Stone of the Joining'. The brothers demand that she seduce the Roman Centurion to find out military information, which is a typical spy story that we see quite commonly today. However, Venetia refuses and invokes her altruistic vows as a priestess. The brothers placate her but, I sense from the way Venetia or Rebecca described their closing dialogue, they will attck the Romans anyway.

"So next we have Elliot's second dream, He has built a garrison on a hill, but it appears he, as well as his men, have lost their military edge. They're lounging when the shocking news comes that the main legion has been ambushed and is now under siege. Celonius snaps out of his peaceful state; his military prowess kicks in, he executes some men who refuse to fight as they too have succumbed to this call to peace. Celonius senses that he has been betrayed by Venetia, he thinks she has cast a spell over him and his men. I need to remind you that the cavalry are the eyes of any army. It is their job to reconnoiter, collect intelligence and report back to the main army headquarters. Apparently, Celonius hasn't carried out his mission and feels he is to blame for the legion's disaster. He plans a diversionary attack on a village not far from the siege to draw the Celtic army away from the Legion, as the Celts will attempt to save the villagers.

"Next we have Rebecca's first dream, Venetia is riding through a village, and there is death and destruction all around her. Obviously, she stands at 'ground zero' in the middle of the Roman attack. Celonius rides up; see's her, believes she has cast a spell on him; she attempts to tell him that, albeit to late, she's there to stop the attack on the legion. Celonius believing she betrayed him, in a rage, attacks her. Does he kill her? Does she convince him of her innocence while he has her pinned to the ground, his gladius at her neck? We don't know."

An abrupt silence fell over us, unable to talk, even think, realizing the enormity of Charles's rendition of my and Rebecca's dream sequence. I stood up and walked over to Rebecca, held her hand and motioned for her to stand. I held her close and tenderly, cradling her head on my shoulder. "I'm so sorry Rebecca, so sorry to have done this to you, to have you in this dilemma." She held me tightly and I embraced her all the more. "Elliot, what are we to do, why is all of this happening," she whispered.

Charles, after allowing our tender embrace, said, "I think we need to talk about this. Yes, why are these dream visions happening now and what are we to do about it. You see, you have both experienced profound flashbacks that have led to amazing archeological discoveries. But I feel we have only touched the tip of the proverbial iceberg. There is more, so much more that awaits us."

"My mother," Rebecca said, "we must go to my mother. Her wisdom goes beyond this world. She holds secrets that have been in our family for generations." "Excellent," said Charles, "As you Americans say Elliot, 'I'm at the end of my rope' trying to figure this out." Still overwhelmed, I could only nod in agreement. Rebecca grabbed my hand; she and Charles led the way through the hotel with me in tow.

CHAPTER 29
Anna Gilcrist

"I've been expecting you," Anna Gilcrist opened the front door just as Rebecca reached for the ornate doorknob. "Mother, we need your help. Elliot and I have had flashbacks to a former life in ancient Britannia and…." "Not here at the front door," Anna motioned toward the interior of the mansion, "in the library."

She led us past the tapestry-covered walls, the ever-changing floor mosaic hallway and into the Gilcrist library. The stacks and rows of books here would rival those of any college library. Anna motioned us to an old but brilliantly finished mahogany round table where cups and a pot of hot tea awaited us.

"Ah, tea, wonderful!" Charles said. "Sit and relax," Anna poured the tea for us. Rebecca spoke first, "Mother, you need to listen to our story. We need guidance on why Elliot and I are having these vivid real life dreams about ancient Britannia and the Roman occupation of Celtic lands." Anna smiled, "Yes, I think I know what you're going to tell me, but go ahead, its best if I hear it first directly from both of you."

The three of us spoke together, Rebecca and I rapidly talking about our visions while Charles, interrupted us to give a summation. It must have been very confusing to hear this entire somewhat disjointed tale. "Stop!" Anna said raising her hand, "you can't all talk at once. Professor perhaps its best if you give a logical summation of the events my daughter and Dr. Rizzo want to tell me."

Charles proceeded to tell, in minute detail and in the proper order, mine and Rebecca's dream visions. Hearing it a second time and a bit more distant from my and Celonius' cave experience, I could see the logic and links within our stories giving them a single thread of continuity. When Charles finished we all sat in silence. The library with its towering bookcases made the atmosphere of silence even heavier. Finally, Anna spoke, "I'm sure you know that your dream visions are not a random set of events brought to your attention without reason. You all have been brought together to correct a wrong that happened two thousand years ago. That wrong, or the massacre of the village along with the attack on the legion, was not supposed to happen."

"But it did happen," I said, "So doesn't that make it right. Not right meaning it was the correct thing to do, but right meaning it indeed happened?" Anna shook her head, "Life does unfold according to a general plan and the plan for that time was the growth of a new culture evolving from a blend of Christian Mysticism along with Celtic beliefs of

God expressing through nature. Alone, each one lacked a certain aspect of spirit that the other could provide. If these two were to unite, which was the purpose of the Stone of the Joining, they would have shown the link between earth and heaven, the spirits of nature and the spirits of heaven. The seen and the unseen are all an expression of the One and revealing to all that 'as above so below' is real. What happened instead, they grew apart; Christianity while giving birth to numerous saints and sincerely religious people became a religion steeped in hierarchy and dogma, Celtic Mysticism waned into repetitive cycles and fertility rituals that were considered pagan and were eventually done away with by the church. Throughout history, there have been great Christians, like St. Francis of Assisi and St. Hildegard of Bingen, who lived the oneness of nature and heaven but not enough to re-ignite the power infused in the Stone.

As she looked at Rebecca, the older woman's eyes soften, "Yes, I've known for some time now that you Rebecca were born unto me as you have been many life times before. But this life of ours together differs from those of the past. This life culminates the others, this life," Anna looked at me, "as you Americans say, 'this is where the tire meets the road.'" "I'll say," Charles said, "the intensity of their dream visions has become more vivid and the message stronger now than ever."

Anna, her demeanor now serious, "Yes, professor, and your role in this has yet to be revealed but believe me when it is, you will see how important you are."

"Now see here Mrs. Gilcrist, I'm just a coordinator here, nothing more," Charles responded. "Nothing could be further from the truth," Anna fired back. "But the matter at hand now concerns Rebecca and Elliot. These battles and the massacre have to be corrected. They occurred because of the ego-centered misuse of the peace energy of the Stone of the Joining. They have blocked the energy of the timeline that was to bring peace to the land, and yes even to the world. The blockage needs to be cleared now so peace will flow again throughout our land and eventually throughout the planet."

"I had a strange feeling this has to do with the Stone of the Joining," I said. Anna looked at me and then to the others, "Exactly, two thousand years ago, at the beginning of the age, two women came together, Mary Magdalene and Laudanae the greatest of all priestesses of all the Celtic Clans. Mary brought the energy of her husband, Jesus representing the Sacred Spirit that resides in us and we in it- the Father God, while Laudanae representing Celtic mysticism, representing the Earth Mother-Goddess who through Her creative nature, gives us and sustains our life. The two joining together would unite spirit and matter, heaven and earth and reveal to all that all are from the same Spirit. They infused their energy into a sacred stone, the sorcerer's stone if you will, to be held for millennia, until the right time, and that time is now." "But what does the massacre have to do with it?" Rebecca asked. "The massacre, its horror, the hundreds of woman and children dying in agony, the death of thousands of Celtic warriors and Roman soldiers has created an energy block that is surrounding the stone. Those women and children ripped from the peace and love of their families and the land were in shock, which prevented them from entering fully into the spirit world. Confused and horrified, they sought refuge in the energy of the stone and their spirits are still there in a sort of tertiary plane between dimensions. This aberration resulted from the misuse of the Stone of the Joining.

"To add to this energy blockage, the violence and destruction followed them, as well as all of the Roman soldiers and Celtic warriors killed in that bloody conflict. So now we have conglomerations of trapped souls, some still fighting, forming this bubble of suppressed energy over and within the sacred cave severely limiting its radiant loving energy. Further still, as a log jam in a river catches more logs and blocks the river further, some souls of those killed in violence in the two millennia since, raging from all of the invasions, the Crusades, feudal wars through World War II and up to today's ongoing conflicts have been trapped in this ever growing maelstrom of blocked energy."

"What!" I said, "What do you mean?" "Yes, mother, please explain and, I must add, you are scaring me," Rebecca said. "My dear, its time you learned of this too as its part of our family heritage. You have been so wrapped up in the business world, there wasn't enough room in your life for this revelation. But the time has come; you have many gifts Rebecca and they are starting to reveal themselves to you now."

Charles leaned back in his chair with an approving smile on his face. Anna added, "but there are three persons missing here who also need to hear what I have to say." "My brothers?" asked Rebecca. "Yes, for they, too, are involved with your story, aren't they my dear?" "Yes, but how do you know?" Rebecca asked. "I know my dear, I have known for ages," Anna said. She picked up an intercom handset from the table next to her, "Steven, the time is upon us, bring Lance and Robin to the library." Her voice now one of authority and firmness, her tenderness gone.

"There are many worlds besides the one we see, hear, touch, taste and smell with our senses. Layers of life surround us beyond our senses and beyond the range of our manmade instruments to detect. Souls on these layers, live, learn and love and then progress to a higher layer." I interrupted, "I presume then that God is on the highest layer?" "God is on every layer," Anna responded with a tone of reverence, "the higher the layer, the more a soul is continuously aware of the Divine Presence. The lower the layer, the greater the influence of the senses, the ego and the mind which has a tendency for its own purposes to block that awareness but the Divine is still omnipresent. Let this information suffice for now."

Steven, Lance and Robin walked into the room. Three solid looking fellows, Robin the fairest, Lance held a sort of military like bearing, Steven, by far the biggest, emanated a soft gentle demeanor.

Anna explained to the brothers, "Dr Rizzo and Rebecca have experienced a series of overlapping dream visions of the past that have had a profound impact on their lives. "You two," she pointed at Lance and Robin, "are a part of their visions and you need to hear their stories. I have told you from your earliest days about how you lived many lives before. Now is the time for you to face the most crucial of all past lives." Both sat back, Robin appeared interested but Lance's, face, although following his mother's directive had an impatient grin. I told my story first to win their interest; I emphasized how my first time travel helped me discover the Roman outpost at the river. They seemed to listen politely but when Charles chimed in to add the significance of that find, Lance's impatience changed to genuine interest. Lance asked questions during my second dream. Celonius' military strategy using a diversionary attack on the village seemed to fascinate him. "Did the diversion work, do you know? Was that in your vision? Brilliant stroke of military genius," Lance said. Rebecca shot back, "Not so brilliant if you were on the receiving end like I was." "Oh?" Robin asked. Which prompted Charles to step in, "Yes, your sister will add much to the story but let Elliot finish."

After I finished my three stories, Rebecca told hers, then Charles summarized. "I have an idea where we fit in," Robin said turning toward his brother. "Really!" Lance shot back, "I think this would make a great fantasy novel but I don't see what it has to do with us." Lance looked over to Anna, "Mother, can you help us with this dilemma?"

CHAPTER 30
The Revelation

Anna looked at her oldest son, Steven, who, up to now, sat quietly. "Put it together mates," the big man said, "why do you think you are here? In all of these stories you've just heard from Rebecca and Elliot, whom do you think manipulated events to cause the attack on the village? Does Rebecca have to repeat her story on how the two of you told her to use her body to get information from the Romans?" "I know where you're driving this," Lance said, "but those were savage times. There were many massacres by the Romans. Why such importance on this one and why drag us through the mud about it."

"There you go Lance," Robin said, "you've nailed it right on. Dragging us through the mud, don't you see we are the ones who egged Rebecca or Venetia to betray Elliot or Celonius and to use the power of the Stone to do it. You realize that don't you? So why are you trying to dodge it?"

Lance lowered his head, "It was hard times, it was war and I suppose we had to do what we had to do. But, then that

Druid kept pushing us on. Right?" "Yes, Lance," Anna said, "but do you see what happened, the Stone, the Stone of the Joining, its power of peace became a weapon of deceit. The Romans had stopped their advance, their exploitation of the land and were ready to start a neutral posture in Britannia, then the attack happened while they had their guard down, settling into this new neutrality. Because of this manipulation of the Stone's purpose, the energy patterns flowing through the Stone became distorted; war again started and the power infused within the Stone started to shut down its peaceful emanations so it could not be misused again.

In a way I could see the logic of Lance's position, "Who's to say the war wouldn't have re-started anyway. How do we know the Stone would have had any influence at all?" "We don't know," Anna replied, "it was never given a chance to show itself fully." "So what do we do?" Rebecca asked. "Can we restore the power placed into the Stone or can it again act as a relay point? And is The Stone of the Joining and St. Leo's Stone one and the same?"

"Of course they are the same, legend has it that St. Leo, or Brother Leonidas his real name, rediscovered it and used it during his life. Some of the power in the Stone still filtered out. Its energy of peace and tranquility synchronized with his simple sincerity. The combination of the Stone's reduced power along with the mystical devotion to God of St. Leo aided in the cure of many of the sick and dying; it helped him in preaching his simple Christianity. As the Romans abandoned the area, Brother Leonidas entered and, somehow stumbled onto the Stone of the Joining. That gave the early Christian church somewhat of a foundation in Britannia allowing him to build a church on top of the Roman ruins on the hill for all around to see."

Anna flashed a look at Charles and me, "all that is left are the ruins at the top of the hill you have been surveying. The so-called 'miracles' he performed through the power of the Stone catapulted him, if I may say, into stardom, throughout Britannia. When the Romans left, the Britons were looking for something to replace them. St Leo finding and using the spiritual energy transmitted through the Stone of the Joining more than filled this need for them."

"So, it sounds like the Christian message wasn't the only reason behind St Leo's success," I asked. Anna nodded, "He lived the message, his sincerity and childlike enthusiasm, made the unblocked energy of the Stone of the Joining that managed to enter our dimension of time respond to him. Remember how the Stone came to be? Even though, its energy became blocked because of the massacre, it did respond to the simplicity of St. Leonidas."

Anna then turned to Charles, her look had more than an inquiring air about it, "Does all of this make sense to you Dr. Weldon?" Charles slowly put his head down and nodded. His body rocked slowly and I could see that a deep emotion ran through him. Of all the years I've known Charles, I've never seen him in such a state. The room became quiet, only Charles' barely audible sobs could be heard.

In what seemed like ages, Charles finally spoke, "Excuse me, please. I'm normally not an emotional man and keep myself well in control. But..." He lowered his head and sobbed more loudly this time. Lance who seemed fidgety throughout the meeting, stared at Charles in a reverent curiosity.

"Can you feel the Stone, Dr. Weldon?" Anna asked. Her gentle yet firm manner brought Charles back to us. I stared at Anna, then to Charles. All in the room, still dead silent, sat in near shock as this mini-drama unfolded. "Never felt so profoundly moved before," Charles' voice quivered, "I'm overwhelmed with joy, awe, peace but these are only words. I don't think I..." then Charles became silent again, seemingly unable to speak anymore.

"You'll be alright Charles. You are one of us; you know that now. Before you played the role as director and concerned observer; it is ok just to sit and process what you're going through," Anna said. Rebecca stood up, went to a pitcher of water, poured a glass full and brought it to Charles.

"And just what is he going through?" Lance asked. Anna replied, "You'll find out soon enough, all of you will, some of you have already, experienced what it's like to recall and feel a past life. You've heard Rebecca's and Dr. Rizzo's stories haven't you. Ask yourself what is your story, why are you here?"

CHAPTER 31
The Battle of Bradene

Lance exhaled loudly, "Mother, you know I live here and I am your son and..." Anna interrupted, "I didn't raise a fool Lance. Where do you fit into this story? Close your eyes, all of you, my boys, be silent, go within yourself." She picked up a brass Tibetan bowl and tapped its side with a wood striker. A sharp musical vibration, amplified by the shape of the room, shuddered through all of us. The vibration continued as she rubbed the striker over the top of the bowl. Its tone blocked out my thoughts and placed me in a restful state of mind.

I peeked out and saw Anna standing, her hands rose over her sons and Charles, slowly swaying clockwise. The four men sat seemingly in a trance. Lance and Robin's face showed a painful grimace while Steven and Charles smiled pleasantly.

After four or five minutes, Steven spoke first, "A remnant of holy Druids who believed in the Stone kept the knowledge and power within the Stone alive. I saw that I was one of those Druid priests. I also protected the cave where the stone was kept from wanderers. The Stone seemed to be losing its power, it radiated love and peace but one had to be closer to it to feel it. The turmoil and fighting throughout the land, fighting with the Romans, the infighting among the clans seemed to block its energy. I then saw myself approaching a cave, which like a mother's womb, held the sacred Stone. I had to protect it from a man who knelt in front of it. With my knife drawn and ready to strike, this man dressed like a Christian, swayed in a sort of ecstasy. I could tell the power of the Stone had somehow touched him. He turned toward me, I saw the joy in his face, the tears of happiness in his eyes, and... and... it was you Charles. Yes, Charles, you are the incarnation of St. Leo."

We all looked at Charles. I felt somewhat confused at his new role, from the all knowing, calm and deliberate professor to this humbled simple soul who had fallen head long into this ever-growing mysterious story. Charles nodded, "yes, yes, I remember, we then became brothers of the Stone. We walked into the cave together. Yes, yes, Steven I remember."

Lance spoke, in an uncharacteristically somber voice, gone were his cynical undertones, "the massacre at the village, I see my role in this now. My God, what did I do?" "I was there too," Robin fidgeted in his chair, "I'm the biggest traitor. I knew of the Stone and I felt its peace. But deep inside of me, another song was singing, one of bravery, of manhood and of fighting. I picked up the sword my father gave me, the sword I thought I'd never touch. It felt good in my hands, balanced, it begged me to swing it, to use it for what it was made for." He sat back, seemingly more at ease with his story, "I started to listen to that strange Druid who came into our the village talking against the Romans, talking of uniting with the other clans and driving them out of our land. It wasn't long before we hatched a plan to strike at the main Roman Legion separated from its cavalry and appearing to have lost its offensive capabilities. They easily became vulnerable to our plan of deception and attack."

Silence ensued. We all looked at the two younger brothers, waiting for their terrifying drama to unfold. Finally Lance spoke, "We got them good, surprised them and surrounded them. Many died before they retreated into a defensive ring a kilometer south of the village of Bradene. Days before we attacked, we hid our shields, swords, bows and spears in the bottom of carts. Rolled them right past the Roman sentries and dispersed them in hiding places in the village. We had more than adequate weapons for our attack. Very few Roman cavalry patrolled the fields and forests at night. In fact, we hardly saw any patrols, a gift given to us to travel in groups at night without detection. The clans crept into the village at night and we dressed for war."

Rebecca pointed an accusing finger at her brothers, "The Roman cavalry sought peace. They were close to the Stone and became peaceful and you took advantage of the Stone and of me. I, the Celtic High Priestess of the Stone, promised them peace as did our elders. You betrayed us all!" I wanted to say something to be a part of this unfolding story some of which centered on me as Celonius. But my time to speak had passed and more of this ancient story had to unfold. I sat in silent observation taking in every word and gesture.

"Yes my sister," Robin spoke softly but with determination. He nodded his head, "we did and many of our men including the elders didn't want to fight either. But a core group of us, Lance and I along with that Druid, shamed them into fighting. We fought the peace of the Stone and, in some way, it seemed to release us. Our addiction to destroy the Romans spread, men joined us, and our plan seemed flawless. Our attack was well executed, the Roman Legion taken by surprise, fell back losing hundreds of men. Victory was within our grasp when it happened, when it all changed."

Charles, long silent, spoke almost as a matter of fact to the group, "I know from Elliot's visions. The Roman Cavalry battle horn sounded and they attacked, hundreds of galloping black horses with men in shinning armor atop of them."

Robin looked at Charles in surprise, "Yes, exactly, and a formidable and awesome sight they made charging at us. The ground shook, the air vibrated and all around the land rumbled from their powerful horses. But we had planned for them; we were ready. We knew that they had to attack either our rear or flanks. We tactically posted archers in key positions to fire into them as they neared us. Those Romans who made it through the barrage of arrows would ride into a barricade of sharpen staves set at the proper angle. The staves would rip into their horse's chests throwing their riders into a second barrier of spear-sharpened staves. Behind that, we dug a trench that any riders who made it through our deadly outer works would fall into. Our warriors stood in rows after the trench, ready to descend on their hapless riders with sword and spear. We would take no prisoners, we would slaughter all of them, the horses included."

Almost on cue, Lance took over the narrative, "They charged with swords drawn, their black horses seemingly snorting out fire, the riders clad in bright armor atop black horses shocked us, they screamed out a staccato of battle cries, a dreadful roar shook the ground as they galloped fearlessly toward us. But our warriors did not waiver. In fact, we stood our ground, raising our swords and beat them against our shields, drumming a heavy resonance in defiance to the intimidating shock and awe of the Roman attack."

"Yes, I felt fear, but our warriors defiance and battle cries gave me confidence. Plus, I knew our defensive perimeter so cleverly placed would decimate the cavalry charge. I snickered inside of myself wondering how the Roman Centurion leading the charge against us could be so naïve to command a direct frontal assault on our position. I secretly thanked the peaceful energy my sister, Venetia, had fostered. It made the Romans oblivious of our preparations for the sneak attack and now, their cavalry blundered toward us, soon to be decimated by our superior tactics and strength."

CHAPTER 32
The Artisans of War

"Then it happened," Robin continued with the story, "as they came within range, and we were ready to give the command for the archers to fire, a Roman battle horn filled the air with a deep dreadful sound. Before our eyes, carried out with admirable precision, the cavalry wheeled sharply to the left, changing the direction of their charge and headed straight north to the village of Bradene. We stared in shock and horror. The fighting adrenaline that coursed through us turned into an overwhelming sense of dread. The village, unprotected, filled with women, children and elders, became the target of the Roman vengeance."

Slowly, holding back tears, Lance continued, "Then we heard a different sound. The thunder of hoof beats subsided when the Romans broke into the village. Terrifying and agonizing screams of the villagers, starting off as a murmur rose to chorus of blood and death. 'They're killing the villagers! The women, the children, the bastards are slaughtering them,' one of the warriors screamed.

"Smoke and flames jutted into the sky. The Romans were methodically killing and destroying the fair village of Bradene. The screams from the dying women being hacked by swords, children being trampled by horse hoofs, elders being dragged by their hair and thrown into the burning thatched huts, rose to an unbearable crescendo of this brutal massacre.

"'My children, my dear children, my wife. No!' A brave village man raised his sword high and he ran out through our barricades toward his village. Another warrior screamed, 'what are we doing here? We must run and save them.' And, without thought or plan, all the warriors ran out through our now useless barricades and through the open fields that led to the burning village. Of course, we fell right into the Roman trap, thousands of disorganized men running without form or military order in an open field, now became our gift to the enemy.

"A second Roman battle horn sounded with two distinct blasts, which, as I see now, was the signal for the besieged Roman garrison to leave their battle works and attack us from the rear. They poured through the barriers, formed a long battle line, swords drawn, shields at the ready and with a steady cadence marched double time toward us. Their archers opened and sent hundreds of arrows into our running mass of men.

"As by a cunning plan, thru the smoke swirling from the village, a line of hundreds of black horses with silver clad armored riders stood a few hundred meters ahead of us. The slaughter in the village continued. The cries of the women and children being ripped by Roman steel begged us to run forward to save them. Behind us, the Legion's war drums beat a double time cadence as the soldiers beat their swords on their steel shields, as they continued their deadly and precise charge toward us. Our leaders saw all of this too late and tried to organize a make shift defensive formation. But it was of no use; we were out maneuvered and trapped by professionals. The Romans were truly the artisans of war."

Racked with emotion, Robin laid his face in his hands, and wept. Lance fought back his emotions and continued in short sentences interlaced with heaves of crying, "I cannot tell you... the feeling of utter helplessness... and despair... of total terror... of imminent death... of screaming babies ... and the beating throbbing cadence of the Roman war drums, the thundering roar of the horses as they charged us..." Lance composed himself to speak of the end in a sort of warrior display of final courage as the discipline learned in this life in the Royal Marines took over.

"...of the panic and screams of brave warriors seeing their families massacred and knowing they too are about to be butchered. But in the final moments, our warrior spirit took hold. We stood our ground, raised our swords and shields, with the hail of arrows flying down on us like a screaming tornado, we turned to face them. Those warriors in the rear faced the advancing Legion. I, and my once innocent young brother, Finian, faced the charging cavalry. And we fought, and we died. Death was merciful, the last I remember, the sounds, the horrible sounds, of war drums, thundering horses, screaming woman and children, yelling soldiers and dying men. You have no idea how hellish and horrific the sounds are on a battlefield."

Letting go of all his control, Lance sat beside his still crying younger brother and embraced him. We sat in utter shock and awe of this horrifying story that happened two thousand years ago told as if it occurred just yesterday. By the grace of God, all remembrance of my role in this slaughter was hidden from me. I had gone through enough past life agonies and so did Rebecca. In some sort of Divine Mercy, we were given the role of spectator and not participants in Lance and Robin's story.

Anna walked toward her two bewildered sons; Steven and Rebecca stood up and rushed to them. They all embraced. "The story has been told," Anna said, "our work can now begin, we can start the healing, clearing the blocks that hide the power within the Stone, the joining of the Father to the Mother."

Charles and I could only nod in agreement not really knowing what she meant but deep down inside, we knew what she said was divinely right.

Epilogue

The back door of the library opened to the manor garden. Sensing the Gilcrist family need for privacy, Charles and I walked out to the garden and sat on an ornate stone chair. Finding it difficult to speak, we just sat and looked out at the garden. Majestic flowers and herbs stood in brilliant colorful rows and sections; a master stone walkway that branched into smaller side paths added to the geometric patterns of this colorful wonderland of nature. Charles took out his pipe, stuffed it with tobacco, packed it down, lit it with a wooden match and started to puff up his typical chimney-like smoke clouds. "You know," he gazed over at me, "Celonius is a dead man." In astonishment I replied, "Really, yes I think he died two thousand years ago." "Ahh, you impetuous young man," he fired back, "you know that's not what I mean. He's a marked man, the Romans will execute him." Perplexed, I replied, "I don't get it. He did save the day, developed an ingenious battle plan, saved the Legion and destroyed the enemy. Celonius is a hero in my book." After a few more puffs, Charles looked at me, "In your eyes, yes, Elliot. But put yourself in Vespasian's place. Think now, carefully. As a General of a battered Legion, which took heavy casualties, how would you view our hero cavalry officer?"

I leaned back, starred out at the rows of the geometrical patterns, and contemplated how it all fell into place, each pattern having its place within the whole complex, "Yes, I understand now what you mean. As you said back at the hotel Charles, the cavalry is the eyes and ears of the army. They patrol, reconnoiter and suppress enemy activity that could threaten the Legion. Under the influence of the peace vibrations coming from the Stone and the authentic overtures of peace from the Celts and specifically, the beautiful and sincere Venetia, he suspended the daily patrols. Their vigilance would have caught the clandestine activity that fueled the attack. He technically is at fault and, with the Legion loosing hundreds of men as well as falling into the Celtic trap, the general would use him as his scapegoat."

"Yes, now you see. Vespasian has no choice. I'm sure after the battle, he would have had Celonius arrested, placed on trial and probably executed or sent back to Rome in disgrace," Charles said.

"Venetia, too, will be marked for death." We turned and there stood Anna and Rebecca. "Quite right Anna," Charles responded as we stood up, in courtesy. "Be seated, Gentlemen," Anna said as both she and Rebecca entered the patio and sat on the last two remaining stone carved chairs. "How are Lance and Robin," I asked. "Steven is attending to them now with his private stock of brandy. They should sleep well tonight," Rebecca said.

I looked at Anna, "Why did you think Venetia is doomed also, Ms. Gilcrist?" "Please Elliot and Charles, call me Anna, our days of formality are over with." I smiled and nodded. Charles puffed more clouds of smoke, which seemed to flow in rhythm with the nod of his head. "As Celonius became victim by the subversion of the Peace from the Stone, so did Venetia. The Village Bradene has been destroyed and hundred of women, children and elders have been brutally killed by the Romans. We are not laying blame to anyone side in this event; everyone has been a victim. All the Celts knew of Venetia's relations with Celonius, the Romans and her orchestration of peace as Priestess of the Stone of the Joining. She will be blamed for the massacre. And believe me, her death by the Druids will be far more torturous and painful than Celonius' execution."

"We're speaking about Celonius and Venetia's plight as if it's going to happen tomorrow, like the next episode in a drama series," I said. "Perhaps it is," said Charles. Rebecca and I looked at Charles and shook our heads but Anna leaned forward, "Yes, Charles please continue." "Look at it this way," said Charles, "Elliot and Rebecca can travel back in the dream state to see and experience what happened two thousand years ago. We need to ask ourselves can they go back perhaps together and maybe influence or change what happened back then?"

In stunned silence we looked at Charles. "Yes Charles I understand," said Anna, "But how do you propose to do that?" "With a simple phone call," said Charles. "Really, and to whom?" Rebecca asked raising her imploring hands.

Charles puffed some more smoke, "why of course to Dr. Dunningham. Who else?"

"And whom, may I ask, is Dr. Dunningham? "asked Anna. I jumped in before Charles could respond, "she is the director of the physics department back at the University." "Ah, yes. Explain please, you definitely have my interest," said Anna.

"She spoke about how quantum physics could explain how we traveled back into the past. At times through a Traversable Wormhole, which would explain the spinning sensation Rebecca. She gave some strong reasoning as well as examples, and I really think she can help us now," I said. "Well that sounds wonderful, can we call her?" Rebecca asked.

"I'm just taking my cell phone out now," said Charles. "I'm sure she will gladly listen to our plight and offer some solutions or direction." "At this late hour?" I asked. "Yes, unbeknownst to you, I met with her when I returned to the University the other day. She has volunteered to be 'on standby' if we need her in any way. I sent her a message as we left the hotel before we came here and updated her on your experiences, Rebecca as Venetia, as well as the latest revelations of Celonius. I've asked her to research how the latest theories of Parallel Universes, dimensions, wormholes and quantum physics may explain these experiences or even be a path to follow."

After a moment of silence, I replied, "A path to follow? Are you suggesting that we go back in time somehow to change what happened?" Charles looked at Anna who smiled and nodded, "Very good Professor, it appears we have the same purpose in mind." "Mother…?" Rebecca sat forward. "How will we do that, all our trips back in time have been random, occurring out of order and at times not of our own choosing. We were 'back-seat passengers' in this vehicle to the past, we were not the drivers."

"Up until now, yes my dear daughter, as passengers, but let's talk to the good Doctor Dunningham for I believe she and I may help to put you and Elliot in the driver's seat."

Printed in the United States
By Bookmasters